HARDPRESS.NET
HOME OF HARD-TO-FIND BOOKS

Corn in the Blade
by Crammond Kennedy

Address:
HardPress
8345 NW 66TH ST #2561
MIAMI FL 33166-2626
USA
Email: info@hardpress.net

Crammond Kennedy

CORN IN THE BLADE

POEMS,

AND

THOUGHTS IN PROSE.

BY

CRAMMOND KENNEDY.

WITH AN INTRODUCTION BY T. B. CONANT.

NEW YORK:

DERBY & JACKSON, 498 BROADWAY.
1860.

CORN IN THE BLADE

POEMS,

AND

THOUGHTS IN PROSE.

BY

CRAMMOND KENNEDY.

WITH AN INTRODUCTION BY C. B. CONANT.

———•••———

NEW YORK:
DERBY & JACKSON, 498 BROADWAY.
1860.

W. H. TINSON, Stereotyper.   GEO. RUSSELL & Co., Printers.

CONTENTS.

———•◆•———

PREFACE.

A PREFACE is too often an insincere apology for what the writer would have done much sooner, if he could have secured the services of a Publisher. The author of this unassuming volume, in presenting it to the public, only does what he has desired and intended to do, and therefore, the brief statement of a few facts will answer his purpose.

In the revisal and arrangement of his compositions, the author has been greatly aided by timely suggestions from his esteemed friend, C. B. Conant, Esq., of this city.

The reader will notice, by observing the dates, that many of the poems, if they can be so called, were written when the author was little more than fifteen years of age. These are but child-like expressions of a child's emotion. If poetry, they are only the poetry of the heart. Their literary quality might be improved, but extensive alteration would destroy their individuality. This accounts for their publication almost in their original form.

Many of the author's compositions have appeared in religious papers. This he regrets, for, even then, by a little exertion, he could have made them more perfect as literary productions. Some may smile, and think that the author will, for the same reason, lament in after years the publication of the present volume. If he improves, he will undoubtedly perceive more clearly, in the future, his present literary shortcomings ; but he must, at the same time, enjoy the consciousness that he made every effort in his power to rid his later productions of errors and inelegances.

If anything in the volume indicates pure or lofty thought, it must be ascribed only to the ennobling influence of the religion of Jesus. Believing that the sole object of every writer should be the accomplishment of good, the author humbly dedicates this little volume to God, his Saviour, with the earnest prayer that its influence may be—a lasting blessing.

C. K.

New York, *May 15th.*

INTRODUCTION.

—●●●—

It was good philosophy of that wise old Pharisee, Gamaliel, when he said to his brother senators: "Refrain from these men, and let them alone, for if this counsel or work be of men, it will come to naught; but if it be of God, ye cannot overthrow it." He spake of the divine claims of certain men, to which, indeed, God bare them witness, with signs, and miracles, and gifts of the Holy Ghost.

But not less in fact, though it may be for common and inferior purposes, is all truth divine, and all vitality the witness of God to His own. Nothing can live long without God's truth in it, for that is the vital principle. Men need take no pains to kill anything, except it be to spare themselves a present nuisance, for if it be contrary to God and nature, it will shortly die of itself. If it be otherwise, it cannot be destroyed.

> " Ever the fiery Pentecost
>   Girds with one flame the countless host;
>   The word unto the prophet spoken
>   Was writ on tables yet unbroken ;
>   The word by seers or sibyls told,
>   In groves of oak, or fanes of gold,
>   Still floats upon the morning wind—
>   Still whispers to the willing mind.
>   One accent of the Holy Ghost
>   The heedless world hath never lost."

This being true, too much anxiety is felt to keep down, or extinguish the utterances of men. Rather let them be heard. If they have a tone that is in accord with the music of the spheres, it will at least chime sweetly, if not loudly; if it is discordant, fastidious Nature will dismiss and forget the sound. Truth watches her children jealously; she is like the harvest-angels, and is continually in the field, dividing the wheat from the tares—this to the garner, that to the fire; she is like the fisher, overhauling his swollen net—gathering the good into vessels, casting the bad away.

It is not always within the power of criticism to decide in advance of the verdict of time, what will live and what will die. This is especially true when the Poet or Prophet speaks. Sometimes a truth, lying quite unsuspected in Nature's lap, is gathered thence by an uncultured hand. Often the finder of the jewel, which shall buy his freedom, knows nothing of its value—it is to him a rude stone—it is no more to his fellows. But he lays it up, and it abides its time, for it is precious, and can afford to wait. To discover the divine mark upon a thing, human insight is feeble enough at the best; while the masses of men are so shackled by customs, or blinded by prejudice, that it is chance if they ever see it. Therefore, let him speak whose thought presses him. It will either die or live, and if it lives, will live upon its own strength, and owe nothing to another hand. There is a galvanism, to be sure, which gives a ghostly motion, but all the life is in the operator, not in the subject; the dead flesh hastes to be carrion all the same.

Guided by this light, which we see shone so clearly almost nineteen hundred years ago, let us also learn, that if any man has a thought or message to his fellows, he has a right to speak it in his own way. To allow him to do so is a wisdom hardly learned. Yet how surely it were wise to give this liberty—how unwise to deny it. Individuality is the right of every man, and if anything valuable to others comes out of him, it is only in virtue of his individuality that it has worth. Strip it of that quality, impress upon it the mark of any other mind, and in that degree do you cut off its chance of usefulness. There are no two souls alike, any more than two leaves, or blades of grass, and in their diversity, God has made them helpful to each other.

It has been somewhat broadly said, but truly in the main, that no man can possibly state accurately the opinions of another. This is readily believed by one who has experienced the difficulty of stating his own, either to his personal satisfaction, or to the understanding of his hearer. If a man has opinions, which seem to him worthy of expression, and sufficient education to make them reasonably intelligible, by all means let him speak for himself. To alter or correct his work is worse than to suppress it, because you impair its self-quality, which is its originality, and serve yourself with neither fish, flesh, nor fowl. Yet how strongly men are bent upon the contrary course. It is difficult to account for the propensity to correct every man's work by some other man's standard, except on the ground of a universal vanity. So it is found that the wisest critics are the most forbearing in this respect.

Given, then, the privilege of speech, and of speaking in our own way, it remains to inquire what limits the speaker should impose upon himself, to insure a decent degree of consistency, usefulness, and good fame, to save himself from the after shame of prematurity, and to be most clearly intelligible to his audience.

It is certainly no good sign when all the opinions which are held in youth remain unchanged in maturer years.

1*

The least that can be said is that their subject has gained nothing by experience. In general, the opinions of men, although most liable to change during the first thirty-five years of life, are never unalterably settled. It is in the power of every man to make these changes upon the advancing scale, and it argues little honest thought, or study, and little gain from experience or observation, if, at forty, his views are not wider, deeper, and more manly than at twenty-five. It has, therefore, passed into a maxim with some, that no man should write a book until he has passed his fortieth year; to which others add, that then he should write but one. It cannot be denied that the world would be the gainer for the observance of both these sayings, so many are the books which should never have been written. Yet if the fear of exposing an immature opinion, and thus incurring the charge of inconsistency in after years, was allowed always to prevail, we should lose one of the most useful and interesting lessons in the spiritual life—the process of the growth of an individual mind.

The statement of large and mature opinions often has upon the mind of a young person the effect of a eulogistic biography—it hinders belief in the one case, as it discourages imitation in the other. The many and successive steps, often up-hill and laborious, which have resulted in the large and philosophical opinions, are not marked out; the ingenuous inquirer must take these steps for himself, or at least must see them indicated, before he can adopt the conclusion. And in character, such many lapses and temptations as were concealed by the partial biographer, although as much a part of the process which made his subject what he was, as his virtues were, enter into the moral history of the reader, also, and their concealment in a model character is especially discouraging.

There is in the impulses of youth a freshness, unreserve,

and honesty, which is not compensated by any degree of experience or accuracy. These are qualities that the world cannot well do without; yet they, too, are lost in the maturer and standard works of the human mind, and, with them, some of the finest perceptions and most delicate tintings which are the fruit of that first and guileless co-working of the heart and intellect.

" Innocence is Nature's wisdom ;"

there is a nearness to divinity which is not reached again, but is rather lessened by every farther step which the traveller takes.

> " Heaven lies about us in our infancy !
> Shades of the prison-house begin to close
> Upon the growing Boy,
> But he beholds the light and whence it flows,
> He sees it in his joy;
> The Youth who daily farther from the East
> Must travel, still is Nature's Priest,
> And by the vision splendid,
> Is on his way attended ;
> At length the Man perceives it die away,
> And fade into the light of common day."

For this gain, it is well to bear with the inexperience of youth, remembering that his garb may be fitted to him, and his manner improved, and that, while this is the lesser and external work, his spirit will never flash so far and clear again as when it freshly sprang from the Creator's hand to " delight and liberty."

It is not claimed, of course, that genius will mark every effort of the youthful mind ; only that, in its degree, these bright and generous qualities will distinguish it. Nor is it

implied that the mind should be stimulated in extreme
youth, either to perpetrate or publish compositions.   As
youth is peculiarly the impulsive period, then, above all
other times, is spontaneity essential.   No young man
should write—much less seek an audience—if he can help
it.   If he must, God give him speed.

Coleridge remarks, that the method of arrangement, in
collecting miscellaneous pieces, is the order of their com-
position.   This is high authority, and when the collection
is complete, or made in mature years, we see the impor-
tance of the suggestion.   Otherwise the mass is chaotic, and
much discrimination and skill will be required to analyze
and arrange it, so that the world may have its uses.   For
how different would be the impression of successive pic-
tures showing the development and growth of a mind into
symmetry and stature, from the misplaced and irregular
workings of the same mind, now moving feebly and
vaguely, and again rapidly and earnestly, alternately bright
and heavy, or prudent and impulsive.

The rule, however, is less important in the publication
of the writings of young persons, because the progress of
the mind, if not precisely by decades, takes periods.   The
changes which occur between the ages of fifteen and
twenty, are not likely to be broad or radical; while those
which occur between fifteen and forty, are in most cases
so great as to make a revolution, or series of revolutions,
in the mind of the subject.   .

The volume to which these remarks are introductory,
is the work of a young man.   Indeed, many of the pieces
date in his boyhood.   The dew of his youth lies upon
them.   This may be a reason why they should not have
been published.   Yet, upon the whole, a different conclu-
sion has been reached, and so they are before the public.
Among these spring-blooms this introduction stands like a

strange tree—as it is, a growth of a different soil. Therefore the writer takes leave to say what he thinks, or as much of that as he deems best, without fear or favor, either of the author or the public.

Crammond Kennedy was born at North Berwick in Scotland, on the twenty-ninth of December, 1842. The acquaintance of the writer with him dates much later. It began in a trifling matter, and has resulted in an intimacy which one party, at least, has no reason to regret. When he was about fifteen years of age, Crammond, having been from early childhood the subject of religious impressions, made a public profession of his faith. This circumstance, one of the most interesting which can take place in any person's history, determined his aims in life. Thenceforth he devoted his strength and talents to the service of that glorious Saviour, whose love had entered into his heart, and made it free, and joyful, and His own possession forever. At this time he was called upon to address a religious meeting. With little preparation and no thought of the tendency of that step, he complied, and upon rising to speak, found the place densely crowded. He had been a member of a debating club, and as the address was expected, his associates were present to hear him. God gave him utterance, and notice being taken of what he said, he was invited to speak in other places. So it came to pass, that he extended his addresses until they took the form of sermons, and he was soon known as "The Boy Preacher." The objections of sober and conservative persons to such a course in so young a man, are not here to be argued against, nor the dangers of so much notoriety to his modesty and solidity, denied. Only this seemed true, that good was done, and the call was so strong that he could not gainsay it. His own mind is clear that God has allotted him to preach the word of life—in that he will persevere. It will gratify those who believe in the need of solid preparation for such a work, to learn that Crammond is a hard student, and that his most anxious friend could not be more solicitous than he is, to lay the groundwork of a thorough education.

No one can glance at these poems without seeing that they are the breathings of a devout spirit. The tenderest sentiments of the writer are interwoven with holy thoughts. This is clearly his habit and delight. It is not an uncomfortable and ill-fitting garment, not an outside tincture, not an unwelcome duty, but the impulse and ingrained quality of his heart. Young persons who have been carefully brought up, often have an imitative and wordy religiousness. God gave Crammond a thoughtful and reverent mind, and although his profession of religion was made no sooner than his fifteenth year, his change of heart was probably so early in life as to be unremembered by him. From his earliest years, with more or less alternation of feeling, with childish struggles against temptation and pride, but with the ceaseless and increasing grace of God, he has advanced in the Christian life.—By these dealings of God with him, the youthful poet had glimpses of the sublimest themes of the imagination, and the finer efforts of his muse are due to their inspiration. Well might the harp that Jesus strung, be struck first and chiefly to His praise.

As to his style, while it is plainly that of a young person, and is marked by occasional redundancy, by some repetitions of pet phrases, and sometimes by too great elaboration of thought, it is perhaps, as free from these and other defects as could be expected.

In accordance with the views expressed in the first part of this paper, we have hesitated to prune the poems much, although they were submitted to criticism with unflinching freedom, believing that it is better to leave them to speak for themselves in their own way. If they servo no better purpose, they will show, hereafter, what the writer felt, and how well or ill he expressed his feelings at this early age. It is quite likely that he will feel more regret for their publication when he looks them over twenty years hence, than then he will need to feel. There is not sufficient gradation of merit to make the order of their composition important to observe in their arrangement. They have been classified, and the dates generally affixed.

Private reasons, honorable to the author, had much influence in determining the publication of this volume. These reasons have prevailed against prudential objections, the force of which he feels keenly enough. To those who know him intimately, his sincere desire for the glory of God and the good of men, and the promise of spiritual advancement which his docility gives, will render this memento volume more interesting and valuable, than either its curiousness as a specimen of youthful talent, or its really marked poetic fancy.

CORN IN THE BLADE.

A CURIOSITY.

The following lines were composed early on a beautiful morning, as the Author, then a child of *eight years*, was walking up and down his grandmother's garden, listening to the songs of the birds, which were hidden in the old, ivy-covered wall, and admiring, in his childish way, the beauties of Nature.

I LOOK around Creation's sphere,
And view Thy works with wond'ring ear.
My heart with melody is filled,
My soul is to the bottom thrilled,
To hear the birds proclaim Thy praise,
To Thee their little voices raise,
To Thee who dwells on high.
Creation is the work of God ;
I will proclaim His praise abroad,
I will affirm His judgments right,
For He is clothed with power and might.

NORTH BERWICK, SCOTLAND, 1851.

DEVOTIONAL PIECES.

THE LOVE OF CHRIST.

The Lord hath appeared of old unto me, saying, Yea, I have loved thee with an everlasting love; therefore with loving-kindness have I drawn thee.—JEREMIAH.

Having loved his own which were in the world, He loved them unto the end.—JOHN.

For He hath said, I will never leave thee nor forsake thee.—PAUL.

FROM EVERLASTING.

I.

BEFORE the Orb of Day his light sent forth,
Or breezes blew from south, east, west, or north;
Before the tow'ring hills had sought the sky,
Or heav'n's blue canopy was stretched on high;
Before the shining stars, like drops of light,
Had twinkled through the gloom of ancient
    Night;
Before the Worlds of Beauty had begun
To wing their rapid circuit round the Sun,
    Christ loved " His own."

II.

When gloom chaotic reign'd supreme around,
Where Nature on Creation's noon was found;

When all the marshall'd armies of the heaven,
That light, for ages now, to man have given,
Were in the dismal shades of Darkness bound;
When Silence deep, unbroken was by Sound;
Yea, when the Suns that scatter light abroad,
Slept, uncreated, in the mind of God,
      Christ loved " His own."

III.

Before Jehovah tuned the seraphs' voice,
Who now in Paradise with song rejoice;
Before the spotless angels round the Throne
Assembled were; when all in Heav'n was lone;
Before was form'd the groundless pit of Hell,
Where spirits lost, and seraphs fallen, dwell,
Environ'd close by flaming walls of fire—
The walls their sin, the flames, Jehovah's ire,
      Christ loved " His own."

IV.

For, stretching back in majesty sublime,
His love anticipates the dawn of Time;
And, all along the boundless, unknown coast
Of vast Eternity, are never lost
Prophetic glimpses of the unseen way,
O'er which the course of our Redeemer lay

To Calv'ry's Cross, from His bright Throne
    above ;
For with an infinite, eternal love,
      Christ loves " His own."

TO EVERLASTING.

V.

When, quaking frightfully, oppress'd by fear,
Th' astonish'd Earth shall rock, as draweth near
The dreadful Day of Doom ; when from his place
The Sun shall flee ; when dark-eyed Gloom shall
    chase
His light away ; when, in the vault of Night,
The Stars shall close their eyes, and never light
The Eve again ; when black the Moon shall grow,
And Darkness reign above, around, below,
      Christ still will love " His own."

VI.

When, silent midst the awful gloom, shall rise
The Throne of God, stupendous in the skies !
When from the Judge effulgent beams shall
    flow,
And scatter darkness wheresoe'er they go ;
When, startled by the Judgment trumpet's
    sound,

All who have slept in death to life shall bound,
And stand before the Throne ; when ev'ry heart
In breathless dread, shall palpitate and start,
   Christ's love will shield " His own."

VII.

When breathing shall be hush'd, and silence
  deep,
And still as death's unbroken, dreamless sleep,
O'er all shall reign, the awful Book of Fate
Will open'd be ; the everlasting state
Of an assembled universe ordained,
And Satan, rampant now, forever chained :
When Christ, the Judge exclaims, in righteous
  ire,
" Depart ! ye curséd, to eternal fire !"
   His love will guard " His own."

VIII.

When, horror-struck, the doomed shall hoarsely
  call,
" Ye rocks and mountains, hear, and on us fall !
Oh ! hide us from the piercing eye of Him,
Who sitteth on the Throne !"   When Hell, so
  grim,
Shall ope his burning mouth, and fiercely cry,
" Ye who are doomed th' eternal death to die,

Enter the drear abode of endless woe !"
When, wailing, into punishment they go,
      Christ's love will save "His own."

IX.

And, when the gates of Paradise unfold,
Disclosing endless streets of glittering gold ;
When, midst the sound of loud, triumphal song,
(Sung by the same angelic, white-robed throng,
Who with the cry made Bethl'hem's plains
      resound,
" To ransom fallen man a Saviour's found !")
Shall enter Jesus, and the ransomed band,
The purchase of His blood, to Canaan's land,
      He still shall love "His own."

X.

God is from everlasting.   Who can trace
The thread of His existence to the place
Where first He said, " I AM ?"   So, not till man
Shows where the being of his God began,
Shall number'd be the multitude of years
In which the wondrous love of Christ appears ;
And, only when the great Jehovah dies,
Shall weeping angels melt with tears the skies,
      Because Christ loves no more !

1859–1860.

THE BAPTISM OF CHRIST.

Then cometh Jesus from Galilee to Jordan unto John, to be baptized of Him. But John forbade Him, saying, I have need to be baptized of Thee, and comest Thou to me? And Jesus, answering, said unto him, Suffer it to be so now; for thus it becometh us to fulfill all righteousness. Then he suffered Him.

And Jesus, when He was baptized, went up straightway out of the water; and, lo! the heavens were opened unto Him, and He saw the Spirit of God descending like a dove, and lighting upon Him. And, lo! a voice from Heaven, saying, This is my beloved Son, in whom I am well pleased!—MATTHEW.

We are buried with Him by baptism.—PAUL.

THE sun was setting, and his last bright ray
Had kissed the cheek of the departing day;
But ere the sunbeam sank to sweet repose,
It glistened on a ripple that arose
Upon the breast of Jordan's hallow'd stream;
The smiling ripple caught, and kept the beam.
The trees by Jordan's banks in beauty grew,
And on the sleeping water shadows threw;
These shadows floated lightly on the wave,
A dreamy, melancholy tint they gave.
The leaves waved in the breeze that softly blew,
And on the river's bosom trembled too.
The day had fled, and yet 'twas scarcely night;

It seemed as if the sun, to hide his light,
Had gone to sleep, and closed his burning eye;
But from his rosy bed, all o'er the sky
The softened radiance of his sleeping face
Had spread, to bless the twilight's vacant place.
And, as the sun sank down, the moon arose,
Arrayed in beauty with the shining clothes,
Which, through the day, had decked the glorious
    sun,
That now his circling daily course had run.
The clothes were trailing robes of purest light,
The sun had left beside the couch of Night.
The evening star shone in a cloudless sky,
And twinkled in the firmament on high;
It seemed to be a glittering, beauteous gem
Just fallen from Jehovah's diadem!
The radiance of the sleeping sun, and star,
And moon, in softest beauty mingled were.

'Twas twilight. Jesus stood in Jordan's wave,
The liquid emblem of His lowly grave.
In thrilling tones the Prophet's voice arose,
And, while it sounds, a waiting angel goes,
And cries to every seraph round the Throne,
"Behold the scene I cannot view alone!"
They come! they come! the unseen, heav'nly
    bands,
And hover o'er the place where Jesus stands!
Silence, as deep as death, all Nature bound,

Her God stood there! she worshipped without
    sound.
And now, Immanuel sinks beneath the wave,
And rises, dripping, from His watery grave:
How emblematic of that blesséd morn
When all the locks of dreadful Death were shorn;
When Jesus rose victorious o'er the tomb,
And from the grave dispersed its ancient gloom;
When Christ in triumph soared above the sky,
And reached His everlasting Throne on high!
The Heavens were opened, and Eternal Love
Appeared in likeness of a snow-white dove;
As through the stream the prophet Jesus led,
It gently hovered o'er His sacred head;
And, lo! a voice was heard, which filled the air,
Jehovah, as His Son, own'd Jesus there,
On Jordan's banks the Saviour to the world,
The Gospel's peaceful banner first unfurl'd;
O'er every land it waves, though Satan tried
To drag it down to dust when Jesus died!
Oh! let us dare to suffer scorn and shame
For Jesus' precepts, and for Jesus' name!
Yea! let us tread the path Immanuel trod,
The path made sacred by the Triune God.

March, 1859.

JESUS IN PRAYER.

He went up into a mountain apart to pray and when
the evening was come, He was there alone.—MATTHEW.
Great is the mystery of godliness.—PAUL.

THE shades of evening wrap the earth
    In robes of sable hue;
The stars shine brightly through the gloom,
    And sparkle in the dew.
The pale rays from the cold, clear moon
    Glide softly 'mong the trees;
The sound of distant waves is heard,
    Borne on the evening breeze.

Upon a mountain's shaded side
    A kneeling form is seen;
A struggling moonbeam seeks the place,
    And shows the Nazarene.
In solitude the Saviour prays,
    And prayer to Him is rest;
His holy soul finds sweet repose
    Upon His Father's breast.

What a mysterious, awful scene
    Is that which meets us there,
In this, the lonely midnight hour,
    When Jesus kneels in prayer!

Ye angels and arch-angels, gaze,
     Down from the heavenly land!
Why, oh! why the bended knee,
     And why the claspéd hand?

Ah! who can tell?   Who will reveal
     What work that night was done?
Who bring to light the sacred band,
     That binds the Three in One?
This is beyond the reach of mind,
     Too deep for thought to sound:
The God we cannot know we trust,
     And at His feet are found.

September, 1858.

CHRIST IN GETHSEMANE.

The Day gave place to Eve, and Eve to Night;
The sun and heat to stars and cooling winds;
Labor to rest, and wakefulness to sleep.
Jerusalem, beneath the Eastern sun,
Had, scorched and thirsty, lain; and panted for
The breezes, which, like cool-breath'd Angels,
    blew
Around the city when the sun had set.
The evening shadows fell, and, one by one,
The stars appeared within the blue expanse,
And sparkled in the undulating waves
Upon the sacred sea of Galilee.
The Moon arose, and shed a flood of light
Upon the Temple, and the lofty towers;
Upon the massive walls, and iron gates.
The scene was wondrous beautiful, and they,
Who saw it, worship'd.
              From the star-lit sky
Shone many a silvery ray, that softly stole
Between the boughs and leaves of every tree,
That spread its branches o'er Gethsemane.
As countless moonbeams glided midst the flowers,
They kissed each drop of dew that nestled there,
And then the tears of Earth, like diamonds,
    shone.

The ripples that arose on Cedron's brook,
Broke with the faintest splash upon the marge,
And gentlest gales the liquid music bore,
And breathed it out around Gethsemane.

Jesus had left His followers behind,
And said : "My soul's exceeding sorrowful
E'en unto death; abide ye here, belov'd,
While I go hence and pray."
                         A Cypress tree
Rose darkly 'neath the moon, and Jesus there,
Beneath its shade, fell on His face, and prayed :
"My Father, if it be but possible,
Let this cup pass away.
                    Nevertheless
Thy will, not mine, be done."
                         Th' astonished stars
Twinkled in upper air; the wond'ring leaves
Each other touched, and rustled o'er His head;
And all the dew-bathed flow'rets silent drooped,
As if they listened ; Nature hearkened then
Unto the wail of Christ's Humanity.
With bloodless face, and agonizing soul,
The Saviour from the dewy ground arose,
And came to His disciples, but they slept.

He sought the Cypress shade again, and moved
By agony whose pangs were never felt
By ruined Man, or fallen Seraphim,

He cast Himself upon the earth, and cried,
" *Let this cup pass away !*" Then slowly rose
Upon His knees, and lifted up His eyes.
The moonbeams rested on His face, and, lo,
Great drops of blood oozed from His pallid brow,
And trickled slowly down his ashy cheeks,
And mingled with the dew ! He prayed again—
His pale, uplifted face, the crimson tears,
And His dread agony of spirit, PRAYED :
" *Let this cup pass away.*"
      The innate God,
In that appalling hour, Humanity
Gave strength to say, " *Thy will, not mine, be
  done.*"

What filled the cup that Jesus quailed to drink ?
Mysterious draught ! 'Twas anguish deep, di-
  vine !"

Before the vision of the Son of God
The Judgment Hall arose ! The crown of
  thorns,
The purple robe, and sceptre-reed appeared !
The scoffing throng that mocked and buffeted !—
The hill !—the multitude !—the rending rocks !—
The Temple's sunder'd veil !—the dark'ning sun !
And, lo ! the Sacrifice upon the Cross,
In blood, and agony, and direst woe,
Before the Son of God's prophetic gaze,
   2*

All   dreadful   loomed,   and   haunted   Him,   like
    fiends !
While, like the densest thunder cloud, appeared
The woe unutt'rable, which made Him cry,
" *My God !   My God !   Hast   Thou   forsaken*
    me ?"

       *   *   *   *   *

An Angel came to strengthen Jesus, and
Gethsemane irradiated was
By heav'nly light; the kneeling form of Christ
Within a glorious halo shone.   He seemed
A warrior wounded, yet victorious,
The Man of Sorrows, and the Son of God !

   1859—1860.

THE CRUCIFIXION.

And they crucified Him, and parted His garments, casting lots, that it might be fulfilled which was spoken by the prophet, They parted my garments among them, and upon my vesture did they cast lots. And sitting down, they watched Him there. . . . . Now from the sixth hour there was darkness over all the land, unto the ninth hour. And about the ninth hour, Jesus cried with a loud voice, saying, Eli, Eli, lama sabachthani?—that is to say, My God, my God, why hast thou forsaken me? . . . . Jesus, when He had cried again with a loud voice, yielded up the ghost. And, behold, the veil of the temple was rent in twain from the top to the bottom; and many bodies of saints, which slept, arose. . . . . Now when the Centurion, and they that were with him watching Jesus, saw the earthquake, and those things that were done, they feared greatly, saying, *Truly this was the Son of God.*—MATTHEW.

I.

THE sun in darkness shrouds himself,
    Obscuring all his rays ;
The quaking earth, astonished, views
    Unparalleled displays.

The graves are opening, and thence
    Cold corses, that have lain
In death's deep silence, re-appear,
    Alive on earth again.

The veil of Israel's Temple rends,
　As if in sore dismay ;
The thunders' roar, and lightnings' flash
　Add terror to the day.

Behold ! on Calv'ry's fatal hill,
　A cross erected stands ;
A God-like form suspended there,
　Of worlds the gaze commands.

Well may the orb of day grow dim,
　Well may the dead arise ;
For earth, and heav'n, and hell, are moved
　When God-incarnate dies !

They've nailed His hands, they've pierced His
　　　side,
　And bruised His noble brow ;
They've mocked, they've scourged, they've cruci-
　　　fied,
　And He is dying now !

" Jehovah ! can this ever be ?"
　The wond'ring angels cry,
" Among the host of heav'n, for Christ,
　Who would have feared to die ?"

Who nails the Lord of Glory there ?
　Who will ? who dare ? who can ?

From hell profoundest, demons cry,
  " We dare not! it is man!"

II.

A radiant halo round the head,
  Pierced by the thorny crown,
Reveals the awful gloom that reigns,
  And shows Jehovah's frown.

It shines upon the hideous forms,
  Who nailed Immanuel there,
While, like incarnate fiends, they show
  Beneath the lurid glare.

The Jewish women near the Cross,
  With eyes upturned, we see;
Their pallid faces, in that light,
  Express their agony.

The multitudes around the hill
  Are almost lost in gloom;
They seem like shades that move within
  A dimly-lighted tomb.

Hark! Jesus cries, " My God! my God!
  Hast Thou forsaken me?"
God heard the cry, and strengthenéd
  His own Humanity.

The blood forsakes His livid face,
   And light fades from His eyes;
But still, Divinity awhile
   The power of Death defies.

'Tis past! the mystic deed is done,   .
   And breathed Christ's latest groan;
'Tis finish'd! an atonement's made,
   And Ruin overthrown!

III.

For whom did Jesus die?   Was't for
   The host, Jehovah's ire
Had swept from heav'n, and doomed to writhe
   In darkness, chains, and fire?

Nay! not for them.   For Satan, then,
   Who in his strength might stand,
If purged from sin, the leader of
   Jehovah's seraph-band?

Nay! not for him.   But Christ decreed,
   (O wondrous, God-like plan!)
To die for them who shed His blood,
   To give Himself for man!

1859–1860.

THE MANIFESTATION.

For ye know that He was manifested to take away our sins, and in Him is no sin.—JOHN.

Scarcely for a righteous man will one die, yet peradventure for a good man some would even dare to die. But God commendeth His love toward us, in that while we were yet sinners, Christ died for us.—PAUL.

O groundless deeps! O depths beyond degree!
Th' offended dies to set th' offender free!
                                        QUARLES.

Abyss unfathomable! Love divine—
As boundless as the attributes that shine,
Harmonious, and glorious, Christ, in Thee,
That meet resplendent in the Deity!
Mysterious love! unsought—supernal,
Uncaused and undeserved—eternal!
Self-sacrificing love! a God in clay,
To want, and woe, to shame, and death a prey!
              O wondrous love of Christ!

Astounding sight! Earth shakes, the Sun grows
        pale,
And Darkness o'er the Vision throws a veil.
The Temple of Jehovah rends in twain,
And saints, long dead, appear alive again.

They stand, near open graves, astonished, still,
And upward gaze, appalled, at Calv'ry's Hill!
    While Nature trembles at the sight,
    And Gloom usurps the throne of Light;
    While massive rocks by fear are riven,
    And Death from his domain is driven,
    Dust crucifies its Animator,
    Yea! crucifies the great Creator!
The creature laughs to see life's Author die,
And echoes mockingly His anguish'd cry.
Yet Christ, the Son of God, who could command
A numberless, all-powerful angel band,
To sweep His vaunting murd'rers from the world,
Who could to deepest hell their souls have
    hurl'd,
Uplifts His beaming eyes amidst the gloom,
And prays for those who make His earth His
    tomb!
Yea, while they mock His agonizing cries,
To save them from the hell they earn, He dies!
Then pale and bloody, He resigns His breath,
And opens Glory's gateway by His death!

October, 1859.

JOY IN HEAVEN.

There is joy in the presence of the angels of God over one sinner that repenteth.—LUKE.

A WAITING Angel saw a sinner pray,
And heard the penitential sob, then plumed
His wings, and flashed, like lightning, through
Ethereal space; and then, ascending to
The highest battlement of Paradise,
He cried, while joy divine beamed in his eyes,
And trembled in the music of his voice,
" Ye ransomed hosts, and Seraphim, give ear !"

The myriads of glorious beings heard,
And ceased upon their golden harps to play,
And all the choirs celestial hushed their songs.
Silence pervaded heav'n. Their eyes were fixed
Intently on the Angel's tow'ring form,
As on the height he stood ; and eagerly
They listened for his tidings from the world.

Erect the Angel stood—his form in light
Was bathed, majestic was his mien—and cried
" *A sinner hath repented of his sin !*
Upon the earth our King is glorified :
Ye hosts of heav'n, rejoice ! ye ransomed, sing !

He who was dead—but lives and reigneth here—
The travail of His soul beholds, and He
Is satisfied. The powers of Death and Sin
Are overthrown. Exultant anthems swell!
Archangels, Seraphs, perfect Spirits, join,
To sound a universal jubilee!
Immanuel reigns, the King of Death and Hell!
Redemption is progressing; strike your harps,
  Ye heav'nly choirs! make heav'n resound with
      song!"

The white-robed multitude, who list'ning stood,
In adoration bowed their shining heads;
And, through the courts above, unbroken waves
Of light effulgent seemed to undulate.
The grand, reverberating hymn of praise
Ascends. The harpers' souls out gush in strains
Of music ravishing. The Angels wave
Vials of odor full. Unnumbered crowns
Upon the golden floor are cast, before
The Throne; while countless throngs seraphic,
And the ransomed sing: "All hail, victorious
      Love!
Redeeming Love! thy conquests bring to light
A glorious Immortality. All hail,
Incarnate Love! thy power hath saved a soul
From Satan's everlasting tyranny,
From woe eternal in Perdition's Gulf.
O Christ, for sinners slain, we worship Thee!

Thou art 'The Wonderful,' 'The Counsellor,'
'The Prince of Peace,' 'The Tried, Foundation
    Stone,'
'The Father of the everlasting age,'
'The Mighty God!' O Christ, we worship Thee!
O 'Word,' who wast with God, and who God
    was,
Thou 'Alpha and Oméga,' 'First and Last,'
Thou, and Thou only, art adored in heav'n!
Jehovah! Thou art worthy to receive
Our homage, to possess eternal power,
With honor, wisdom, and immortal praise!
      Alleluia! Alleluia! Amen!"

January, 1860.

GOD.

Art Thou not from everlasting, O Lord, my God, my
Holy One?—HABAKKUK.

Before the mountains were brought forth, or ever Thou
hadst formed the earth and the world, even from everlast-
ing to everlasting, Thou art God.—DAVID.

Thou art unmade—time never was
    When Thou didst not exist;
Thou wast before the hills were formed,
    Or dew-drops flowers had kissed.
When Earth was one chaotic mass,
    Before the sun had shone;
When Satellites and Stars were blanks,
    Thou wast in space—alone!

Before the "blue ethereal sky"
    The void on high adorned,
Thou wast the same, and, in Thy mind,
    All things that are were formed.
Ere Sound was heard, when Silence reigned
    Supreme o'er all abroad;
When mother Earth was yet unborn,
    Thou didst exist, O God!

No Past to Thee; no looking back
    Along the pathway trod;

Thy mind is one, eternal *Now*,
   So vast art Thou, O God!
Unchangeable! Thou canst not change!
   Of wav'ring not a shade
Affects Thy plans; Thy purposes
   Firm as Thy Throne are laid.

All things terrestrial fade away,
   Earth's beauties all must die;
But Thou, O God, shalt ever be,
   And ever reign on high!
When Suns and Planets, Moons and Stars,
   With all the world abroad,
Have passed away, still Thou shalt be,
   To everlasting—God!

', 1858.

GLORYING IN THE CROSS.

Place a crown of gems on my brow, array me in robes of royalty, put a sceptre in my hand, seat me on a throne, and let a nation obey my nod. Empower me to chain the winds, and to hush the tumult of the waves. Let the lightning and the thunder be subject to my control—make me king of the elements. Endow me with an intellect between that of the highest archangel and the Deity, Himself. Give me ability to alter and re-arrange the course of the unnumbered worlds that roll in the infinity of space. Let me form universes by a wish, and kindle suns by a desire. Let all created intelligence, the inhabitants of earth, and the hosts of heaven, adore me. Then, in the plenitude of my power and majesty, let me think of Jesus, "who loved me and gave Himself for me," and, while my soul is inundated by a gush of gratitude and love, I would cry, "God forbid that I should glory save in the Cross of my Lord Jesus Christ!"

Exalt me to a position almost equal to that of the Eternal Son of God. From this sublime height, let me survey my dominions—number the suns with their stars, and the inhabitants thereof. Let me count my angel-servants and gather the cherubim around me. Then, O once crucified, but now exalted Jesus, look down!—tell me that Thou didst die and bear the wrath of Heaven, that I might escape the pangs of hell, be freed from sin, and saved in glory—show me the mark of the spear in Thy side, the print of the nails on Thy hands, and the impress of the thorns on Thy brow—and, oh! my precious Saviour! forgetting the vastness of my power and the glory of my dominions, I would shout, as I beheld Thee, "God forbid that I should glory save in Thy cross, O Jesus, Saviour of my soul!"

Let atheists and skeptics proudly scorn
The Christian and the Author of his faith,
We, who have felt the Gospel's hallowed power,
Will glory only in the Cross of Christ.

Although the bodies of the boastful Paine,
And proud Voltaire, by worms have been de-
  voured ;
Though men, like them, existing now, cry out
'Gainst "superstitious creeds" in "Reason's
  Age ;"
Though haughty Rome into oblivion
Hath, with the ages, gone ; though Empires sleep
Within eternal gloom ; though crowds of kings
Have crumbled into beggar's dust ; and though
A host of centuries have glided by
Into the boundless, past Eternity,
Of which Jehovah is the Fountain-Head,
Yet, O immortal cross ! thy power is felt,
To-day, e'en while I write, upon the earth,
In Highest heaven, and in profoundest Hell !

When, on account of guilt, a sinner weeps,
The people of the Lord, on earth, are glad,
The Angels, and the Church triumphant, round
The Throne of God, exceedingly rejoice,
While Satan, and his foul, hell-born array
Of demons, rage, and tremble, and believe.
  1860.

THE TWO LOVES.

How the divinity of the Saviour's love is manifested when we contrast it with the apparent love of men! The latter is often only the development of hypocrisy, selfishness, or passion. The former is uncaused and undeserved, yet infinite, eternal, self-sacrificing, and unchangeable.

ALL earthly love doth change and fade,
    Like summer flowers;
'Tis fickle, false, and only lasts
    A few short hours.

It wreathes around the tender heart,
    With fibres strong,
Then leaves it desolate, to sing
    A mournful song.

'Tis sweet to be belov'd, and sweet
    Love to return;
But blooming roses 'neath their leaves
    Oft hide a thorn.

And even if it were not so,
    We still must mourn,
For cherished objects from our grasp
    By Death are torn.

I know a never-changing Friend,
    Always the same;
He loved before the dawn of time,
    Christ is His name.

He loves me now, and ever will,
    While ages roll;
For me He shed His precious blood,
    He saved my soul.

When, silent, cold, and motionless
    In death I lie,
His love will bear my spirit up
    To joys on high.

Oh! then in Paradise I'll join
    The sacred throng,
The ransom'd hosts, who sing His love—
    A ceaseless song!

December, 1858.

WHY HAST THOU NO FAITH?

Consider the lilies of the field how they grow; they toil
not, neither do they spin.   And yet I say unto you that
even Solomon in all his glory was not arrayed like one of
these.—JESUS.

My soul, God guides the crystal rain
    That falls on drooping flowers;
He cheers each blade of grass with dew,
    That shines in star-lit hours.

His eye regards the lily's growth,
    And scans the "milky way;"
To Him an hour's a thousand years,
    Eternity a day.

He guides the course of circling worlds
    Around unnumbered suns,
And scoops the gurgling streamlet's source,
    That through the valley runs.

He views the mighty angel-host
    Who bow before His throne,
And when a little sparrow falls,
    To Him its death is known.

He is arrayed in majesty,
    Eternal glories meet

Above His throne, and lo! they form
  A rainbow round His feet;

And yet He numbereth the hairs
  Upon His children's head;
And oh! how precious in his sight
  Are all His chosen dead!

Art thou not better than the birds
  That fly upon the air?
Than lilies of the vale? *They* are
  The objects of His care.

Be still, my trembling heart! Why fear
  When waves of sorrow roll?
Canst thou not trust the love of Him
  Who died to save thy soul?

Survey the handiwork of God,
  Observe his minute care;
And, if a single doubt remains,
  Uplift thy soul in prayer.

October, 1859.

I'LL TRUST IN GOD.

Though He slay me, yet will I trust in Him.—JOB.

For I am persuaded that neither life, nor death, nor angels, nor principalities, nor powers, nor things present, nor things to come, nor height, nor depth, nor any other creature, shall be able to separate me from the love of God, which is in Jesus Christ my Lord.—PAUL.

THOUGH fondly-cherished hopes are blighted,
That once my dreary pathway lighted,
And though I grope in gloom, benighted,
    I'll trust in God.

Though sorrows gather darkly round me,
A contrast to the joys that bound me,
Though fiery trials do astound me,
    I'll trust in God.

Though want and woe, combined, attack me,
Though ev'ry grief, united, rack me,
Though doubts and fears, like armies, sack me,
    I'll trust in God.

Though long-continued sickness pain me,
Though of my health and hope it drain me,
Though with the hue of death it stain me,
    I'll trust in God.

Though all my earthly riches fail me,
Though "summer friends" forsake and rail me,
Though Satan and his host assail me,
   I'll trust in God.

My Saviour with me sympathizeth,
My every groan to Him ariseth,
To cleanse and save me He deviseth;
   I'll trust in Him.

From Jesus nothing can me sever,
Desert, or fail me He shall never,
I'm His to-day and His forever;
   I'll trust in Him.

April, 1860.

SABBATH EVE.

The following lines were composed at the close of a
lovely Sabbath day in the month of September, on the
banks of the lonely and romantic Saguenay, which flows
from Lake St. John, through an uninhabited and moun-
tainous region, into that most majestic of rivers, the mighty
St. Lawrence.

'Tis Sabbath eve, and all is still and calm—
As calm as he whose spirit rests in God,
And never doubts his Heav'nly Father's love.
The soothing sound of rippling water falls
Upon the ear. The soft and balmy air,
With cool and gentle touch, doth kiss the brow,
And plays with fingers soft among the hair.
It waketh holy feelings in the heart,
And sheds celestial peace within the soul.
The clear blue sky, adorned with snowy clouds,
In beauty stretches o'er the tranquil earth,
And bows upon the distant mountains blue.
The waveless water, shaded by the hills,
And brighten'd by the setting sun, reflects
The image of the azure sky.
     'Tis thus,
My soul, thou should'st reflect in holy deeds,
All prompted by the love thou bear'st to God,
Thy Saviour's character divine.

                              The sun
Gilds every cloud with crimson hues, and throws
A track of silver light across the bay,
And sheds a flush of glory o'er his couch
Behind the hills.
                      If thou hast faith in Christ,
Like to the setting sun thy death shall be;
For Faith dispels the darkness of the tomb,
And o'er Death's stream a flood of glory sheds,
That shows the Christian's pathway into heav'n.
Not so the skeptic's death.   His exit from
This life is wrapp'd in gloom, and not a beam
Of light irradiates his grave.   How dark
And hopeless such a tomb! The Christian's faith,
As an illusion, is more glorious far
Than Infidelity, e'en if 't were true.
When Christians "fall asleep," the cheering hope
Of future glory, like the ev'ning star,
That speaks a morn, appears among the clouds
That shade the close of life, and whispereth
Of Immortality.
                      The sun has set,
And twilight shades are falling on the hills,
While Nature has a thoughtful, dreamy look.
The stars peep through the sky, to see if night
Has come.   The moon's pale, shining face ap-
       pears
Beneath a fleecy cloud, and countless stars
Are sleeping in the waters blue.

Silence
Unbroken, save by rippling music low,
Speaks to my soul, and whispers, " Worship God.
He made the sun whose glory makes the Day ;
He formed the stars whose beams illume the
          Night ;
He is the Source of Life ; thine intellect,
With all its faculties, He did bestow,
That thou His praise and glory shouldst proclaim.
Thy heart, with all its sympathies, He gave,
That thou His love and mercy shouldst declare.
Thine eye beholds the beauty of His works,
The grass, the buds, and blossoms of the Spring,
The fruit, and foliage, and sky of June,
The Autumn forests clad in leafy robes,
Made bright, and rich, and sad, by gorgeous hues,
The Winter's icicles, and fields of snow,
The rising, noonday, and the setting sun,
The Midnight's blue, ethereal plain,
Where shines the Moon among the stars that
          burn,
Till in thy soul immortal thoughts arise,
That struggle for expression earnestly.
And when in burning words thy thoughts ap-
          pear,
How deep the joy ! how soothing the relief !
'Tis God who gives expression. Speak of Him.—
Be faithful to thy trust, for thou art watched
By clouds of heav'nly witnesses unseen.—

Be faithful, and thy soul shall never die,
But in the world of thought shall live and act,
When to the dust thy body hath returned.
When crowns have fallen from the brows of kings,
And empires passed away, still shall the power
Of holy influence, increase as time rolls on.
In likeness of a wid'ning, deep'ning stream,
That floweth onward to the ocean's depths,
Thine influence, a mighty sea at last,
Shall roll upon the shores of Paradise,
And on its tide bear thence a host of souls
Redeemed from sin and hell by Heav'n through
    thee.

Thou and thine influence immortal are;
Then to thyself, and to the human race,
And to thy God endeavor to be true."

I hear the distant sound of holy song
Ascending from the cottage near the hill,
And breaking on the stillness of the night.
My deepest soul is moved.   This solemn vow
With the uprising hymn of prayer ascends:
To Thee, O God! to man, and to myself,
I will in thought and action faithful be.

The night's advancing, and my thoughts still
    flow,
While silently my raptured eye beholds
The deep'ning beauty of the lovely scene.

The darken'd outline of the rocky hills,
That gird the lonely Saguenay, appears
In solemn beauty.   The river's course is seen
Among the moonlit mountains, flowing to
The East.   'Tis like a strip of polished steel.
The moon is ruddy, and her face half-hid
Beneath a purple cloud.   She sheddeth forth
Cold rays of light, that mingle with the gloom
Above the rugged rocks and tow'ring peaks,
Where man hath never trod.   No voice, save
     God's,
Which speaks in thunder-storms, that mutter
     hoarse
Among the hills, and echo loudly through
The unexplor'd defiles, is ever heard.
The deep, " mysterious " Saguenay is oathed
In mellow'd light, and awful silence reigns.

HA! HA! BAY, *September*, 1859.

THE PRESENCE OF CHRIST.

The assurance of the Saviour's love is the fountain of peace that passeth understanding, of consolation which the world cannot give or take away, and of joy unspeakable and full of glory. This assurance constrains us to regard every trial as a disguised blessing, death as an angel darkly robed, and heaven as a glorious reality. A want of confidence in Jesus is the source of an anxiety which mantles Christianity in gloom, of a fear which engenders misery, and of foreboding which makes life burdensome, death dreadful, judgment terrible, and eternity appalling. Oh! how supremely desirable to live the life of faith in the Son of God!

O Jesus! Thy smile to my soul
    Is the sun to the day,
    That disperses the gloom
    With its gladdening ray.
Without it, my soul is baptized
    In the depths of despair,
    But my sky is serene
    When thy smile shineth there.

O Jesus! Thy love to my heart
    Is the moon to the night,
    That illumines the earth
    With its silvery light.
Without it, in darkness and fear,
    Oft I wander and fall,

Till Thine accents I hear,
Like a fond mother's call.

O Jesus! Thy presence to me
Is a heaven below;
When I feel I am thine,
Joy of angels I know.
But oh! when Thy presence withdraws,
How appalling the gloom!
Darkness shroudeth my soul
In a desolate tomb.

Then, rise on Thy glorious wings,
Sun of Righteousness, rise!
Be the life of my soul,
And the light of mine eyes.
Immanuel! reign in my heart
O Immanuel, reign!
Till the vict'ry is won,
And the enemy slain.

O Jesus! to Paradise then
Undefiled I will rise,
And lean on Thy bosom,
And look in Thine eyes.
My Saviour! whom have I but Thee,
On earth, or in heaven?
I sinned, Thou atonedst,
And I am forgiven.

February, 1859.

PRAYER.

I.

HUMILITY AND CONFIDENCE.

We should remember when we pray, that we are addressing God. This is often forgotten, and we, therefore, frequently engage in our devotions without feelings of solemnity and awe. We should, also, in order to pray humbly, contrast ourselves both with what we ought to be, and with Him whom we worship. The need of Christ should be vividly realized ; His proffered mediation gratefully accepted, and implicitly trusted. This truth is clearly enunciated in that timely work, *The Still Hour:* "Christ, as the Atoning One, must be a *reality* to the soul, or prayer cannot rise to its full growth, as an experience of blessedness in the friendship of God."

My soul, with reverence approach
The audience-chamber of thy God ;
The place is sacred, awful—none
With thoughts profane, its courts have trod.

Remember who, and what thou art,
Behold the marks of guilt within ;
While seeking God, consider, that
He drew thee from the pit of sin.

Upon His glorious character,
His might and wisdom, ponder thou;
Think of his perfect holiness,
And, in profound abasement, bow.

In Jesus trust, who died for thee,
And who is now thy Priest and King;
And, save the merit of His death,
No plea for heav'nly favor bring.

Thus, humbly, yet with confidence,
Thou shalt in prayer to God draw near;
Thou'lt find it truly blest to pray,
And Jesus will rejoice to hear.

I I.

DEFINITENESS AND DESIRE.

We lose many prayers for the want of two things which support each other—*specificness of object and intensity of desire.* . . . . Let a man define to his own mind an object of prayer, and then let him be moved by desires for that object which *impel* him to pray, because he cannot otherwise satisfy the irrepressible longings of his soul; let him have such desires as shall lead him to search out, and dwell upon, and treasure in his heart, the *encouragements* to prayer, till his Bible opens of itself to the right place—and think you that such a man will have occasion to go to his closet, or come from it, with the sickly cry, "Why, oh! why is my intercourse with God so irksome to me?"

Such a man *must* experience, at least, the joy of uttering hopeful emotions which become painful by repression.— *The Still Hour.*

When unto Christ the ruler came,
His spirit breathed unuttered groans,
And pleaded through his earnest eyes,
And supplicated in his tones.

" *My daughter!* MASTER!" three short words—
The trembling voice of hidden strife—
The soul of Jesus moved, and He
Restored the ruler's child to life.

Pray with *desires* within thy soul,
And fear not though thy words be few ;
God never listens to thy voice,
He hearkens only unto *you.*

Thy wishes search, and know that they
Are all unselfish, true, and pure ;
Then yield them to thy Saviour's care,
He pleads for thee, an answer's sure.

Thy prayers will then be each a *power*,
To move Jehovah's heart and will ;
Thy holy wishes hidden links,
Uniting earth to Zion's Hill !

April, 1860.

DEATH.

While the Bridegroom tarried, they all slumbered and slept. And at midnight there was a cry made, Behold the Bridegroom cometh!—MATTHEW.

So teach us to number our days, that we may apply our hearts unto wisdom.—PSALMS.

THE world's a peopled burial-ground,
The dying and the dead abound;
The quick among the dead draw breath,
Yet *die without a thought of death!*
We gaze upon a marble brow,
And o'er a rigid corse we bow;
We look upon the glassy eye,
Then shed a tear, or heave a sigh,

To think the voice we loved, no more
Will greet us as in days of yore;
To think the footstep, known so well,
Of glad return shall never tell;
But do we pause and think—" Death must
Consign *me* also to the dust;
I must, like him, lie cold and low,—
Am I prepared with Death to go?"

If some one from another sphere,
Should on this earth of ours appear,

And view the laughing, thoughtless crowd,
Rush, heedless, to a common shroud,
He would believe each mortal thought,
"*I* have from death a ransom bought,
And though my friends and neighbors die,
Yet many live, *and so shall I!*"

Our Father and our God, we pray,
That thou wilt teach us, day by day,
To think of death, of heaven, and Thee—
To live for Immortality;
That all our lamps, well-trimmed and bright,
May cheer our souls in Death's dark night;
That when we hear the " Bridegroom's " cry,
We may have naught to do but die.

November, 1859.

BIRTHDAY MEDITATIONS.

Birthdays are milestones on the road of Time. This road leads through the Valley of Death to the Judgment Throne on the margin of Eternity.

If you are young, how appropriate that you should sit down on the milestone, and, uplifting your eyes from the vanities of the world, exclaim, "My Father in Heaven, be Thou the Guide of my youth!"

Pause, if you have reached maturity. Regard your past life, and the results of your existence. Consider the future. Think of death, judgment, eternity, and God. Remember that the journey of life is more than half completed, and that you soon must enter upon the unknown realities of the world to come. Now inquire, "Am I at peace with my Maker, through faith in the atonement of the incarnate God?"

Are you an aged pilgrim on the road to Zion? Then, lean on your staff, and think of the promises. Divinity breathes in this precious assurance: "Even to your old age I am He; and even to hoary hairs will I carry you: I have made, and I will bear; even I will carry, and will deliver you." Jesus speaks, and speaks to you in this consoling promise: "When thou passest through the waters, I will be with thee; and through the rivers, they shall not overflow thee; when thou walkest through the fire, thou shalt not be burned, neither shall the flame kindle upon thee. For I am the Lord thy God, the Holy One of Israel, thy Saviour."

A YOUTHFUL traveller hath reached, to-day,
A finger-post on life's uneven way,
Which pointeth back to birth, and on to death,
Which tells the years since first he drew a breath,
But showeth not the time 'tween him and death.

I have a year the less on earth to be,
Mine eyes another year the less to see;
My brain that space of time the less to think,
My soul another year the less to drink
Deep draughts from Inspiration's sacred well,
Where truths eternal and immortal dwell;
True knowledge from Creation's wondrous book,
Which prompts for the Invisible to look,
Whose attributes are never known aright,
Save in the rays of Revelation's light.

The Past is pass'd, the Present only's mine,
For Death upon my pathway flies behind;
And I rush downward to an open grave,
As on the tempest speeds a foam-capp'd wave!
Most solemn thought! E'en while I live I die;
My life's a rose whose charms attract the eye,
Whose leaves, to-morrow, scatter'd, wither'd lie!
A life of joy is but a fleeting day,
From an eternal sun a transient ray!
A life of care is but a deep-drawn sigh,
For liberty a captive-spirit's cry!

A life of mingled happiness and woe 's
A passing cloud in which a rainbow glows!

Jehovah! may I now my heart apply,
To know Thee, as a Saviour, ere I die,
That from the "wrath to come" my soul may fly,
And live through all eternity thereby,
Unlike the souls who would, but cannot die,
And both in ~~earth and heaven~~ Thee glorify.

Thou art life's Fountain, I a trickling rill,
Meand'ring down the side of Time's steep hill!
Thou art Eternity, I but a day,
Yet hearken, for Thy Son's sake, when I pray!
Until the day of death, O may I strive
To make the world believe I am alive!
Alive, to sympathize with men who groan
In honest poverty and grief—alone;
Alive, to utter hopeful words of cheer
Which downcast mortals shall rejoice to hear;
Alive, to wipe away the orphan's tears,
And soothe the broken-hearted widow's fears;
Alive, to join in every effort made
The cause of Truth and Liberty to aid;
Alive, to stem transgression's mighty flood,
That bathes our universe in vice and blood;
Alive, to dissipate the gloom of night,
Diffuse the radiance of celestial light,

Disseminate the precepts of Thy Son,
And bless the world until my course is run !

O God, bestow what for myself I crave,
And from the power of sin Thy people save !
Then, Satan, angels fallen, heav'nly hosts,
Will feel that Christians are not myths or ghosts,
But living, acting, mighty sons of God,
Who tread the pathway that their Saviour trod !
Then all the world in love shall worship Thee,
Through Christ our Lord.   Amen.   So let it be !

December, 29th, 1859.

PIECES ON NATURE

THERE IS A GOD.

For the invisible things of Him, from the creation of the world, are clearly seen, being understood by the things that are made, even His eternal power and Godhead.—PAUL.

The fool hath said in his heart, "No God."—SOLOMON.

GOD wove each tiny leaf,
Each op'ning bud, and blooming flower;
Each breeze that fans the brow of earth,
  Proclaims His wondrous power.

God reared the mountains grand,
The tow'ring hills that proudly rise
In forms majestic o'er the clouds,
  To greet the spreading skies.

God holdeth in His hand
The thunder loud, and whirlwind strong,
That bear destruction all abroad,
  With anthems loud and long.

God guides the lightning's flash,
That darts, like thought, across the skies,
That, dazzling, shines from east to west;
  At His behest it flies.

4

God calléd to the depths;
They flowed together at the sound;
They roared and raged; they foam and swell;
    He kept, and keeps them bound.

God made the beauteous Moon,
That floods the night with radiance pure,
That bathes the world in silv'ry light;
    Her course he 'stablished sure.

God lit th' effulgent Sun,
On Nature's birthday, with His eye;
He keeps it burning by His breath,
    Within the boundless sky!

The blue expanse of Eve
God studded with the twinkling star;
He breathéd; lo! the "Milky Way"
    Spread out in space afar!

All Nature I survey;
Where'er I look I still behold
Assurance of Primeval Cause,
    Uncauséd and untold;

While in the Book I read,
That he who views vast Nature's rule,
And yet asserts that God is not,
    Must surely be A FOOL.

1859–1860.

THE CONFLICT BETWEEN LIGHT AND DARKNESS.

. . . Darkness was upon the face of the deep; and the Spirit of God moved upon the face of the waters. And God said, Let there be light, and there was light. . . . . . And God called the light, Day, and the darkness He called Night. And the evening and the morning were the first day.—GENESIS.

SILENT through the gloom of chaos,
    Stole the pristine sunbeam's ray;
Smiling sweet, it kiss'd the Darkness—
    Darkness blushing, turned to Day.

Midnight threw her sable mantle
    O'er the face of new-born Sun:
Among the clouds the Moon appearing,
    Hoped that Light had victory won.

Bright-eyed Sun the Moon regarded,
    (Darkness was too blind to see)
Smiling then, her face he lighted,
    Gloom afraid began to be!

Paler grew the Moon while viewing
    Dismal plains where Gloom abode;

Thus she pondered, "Shall the Darkness
    Veil the light the Sun bestow'd?"

Thoughtful stars in silence wonder'd,
    Each one op'd her shining eye,
Till a host of sparkling jewels
    Twinkled through the dusky sky!

Darkness could not bear these glances,
    Piercing through his inmost soul;
Gath'ring up his sable garments,
    From the conflict Darkness stole.

"Victory!" sang the hosts of heaven—
    "Victory in the midnight hour!
To the world, by God created,
    Light hath shown her glorious power!"

The "lesser lights" on Earth's birth-night,
    Fought and conquer'd Darkness blind;
For ev'ry night you may behold
    The shadow Darkness left behind!

HA! HA! BAY, *September*, 1859.

SUNSET ON THE OCEAN.

A scene from the deck of the steamship Alabama, off the coast of South Carolina, May 25th, 1859.

'Tis a calm summer eve, and the glorious sun
Bows his head on the sea, his course being run;
The blue waves beneath him unceasingly roll,
Like an ocean of thought o'erwhelming a soul!
He looks like an angel—an angel of light—
With pinions unfolded all radiant and bright;
While they, in their beauty, spread glory abroad,
On an altar of crimson he worships his God!

The scenes all around him in loveliness glow,
The ripples are lit as they murmur below;
And the dark clouds of purple are fringéd with
    light,
Forming curtains to hide the sun's chamber at
    night!
All glorious he sinks to his bed in the sea,
To the bosom of Ocean inclaspéd is he;
His bright wings are folded, he's pass'd from my
    sight,
And his couch is enwrapt in the shadows of
    night.

I thought as I gazed, " It is thus too with man,
His birth is the sunrise where being began ;
His childhood is morning, his manhood, noon-
      day ;
His death is the sunset, when life's closing ray
Streaks the sea of existence with flickering light,
As a glimmering star the gloom of the night,
Till the shadows of death do extinguish the flame,
Then being is ended, and life's but a name !"

This dark thought o'erpowered me—I then looked
      above—
Stars twinkled in blue, each an emblem of love !
The beautiful moon o'er the sky softly stole,
And silently whispered of hope to my soul !
Thus faith in the Saviour, and trust in His might,
Floods the valley of death with a radiant light ;
For Faith, like the stars that dispel the night's
      gloom,
A halo of glory sheds over the tomb !

SPRING.

KING FROST and King Sun are at war on the
    plain,
And North winds, for King Frost, their energies
    strain ;
But, aiding the Sun King, South breezes come
    nigh,
And draw out a tear-drop from Frost-Monarch's
    eye !

The Sun streameth down on his white, frozen
    head
Him South winds caress on his fleecy snow-bed,
Till now by their fervor his spirit is thrilled—
With heat from their touches his icy soul's filled !

His cold heart is melted, and now, through the
    vale,
It gurgles in streamlets, the earth to regale ;
The streams become torrents which nothing re-
    strains,
For Winter's heart rolleth, to melt Winter's
    chains !

Behold the white mountains and snow-covered
        hills
Become the great fountains of thousands of rills!
If Winter were weeping on each frozen peak,
Pray, what better witness of grief should we seek ?

Now all the dense forests, that, in the moonlight,
Stood silent and ghostly, enshrouded in white,
Have all their bare branches with liquid drops
        hung,
Like jewels on dry twigs by queer fairies strung !

The rivers, from fetters of Winter set free,
Flow, brightly and breeze-ridden, down to the
        sea ;
The ripples, unfrozen, break soft on the shore,
In liquid tones singing, " Oh, no ! Nevermore !"

The green grass beneath me, the blue sky above,
Speak unto my vision of wisdom and love ;
The delicate flowrets upsprung from the sod,
Are unto mine eyesight, fair footprints of God !

The Sun and the South winds, victorious in
        strife,
Thrill Earth, Winter's old slave, with Liberty's
        life ;

And change his cold fetters to nourishing streams,
And fan him with breezes, and warm him with
  beams !

My soul was a captive, and Satan its King ;
Christ freed me, forgave me, changed Winter to
    Spring !
I look for a Summer that never shall die,
Jesus' presence its Sun, and *His* love its sky !

April, 1860.

THE EVENING SKY.

THE sky was like a waveless sea,
    A sea of deepest blue,
From out the limpid depths of which
    Shone gems of radiant hue.

The sky was like a curtain stretched
    Above the silent world.
The Seraphs had, beyond the earth,
    The flag of heav'n unfurl'd.

The unseen forms of angels lay
    Over the jewell'd skies,
I knew they looked at me, because
    I *felt* their starry eyes!

A cloud, as white as snow, arose,
    And floated on the air,
It sought the highest heights of heav'n,
    Like a believer's prayer.

Ascending slow, it wooed a star
    Into its pure embrace;
I thought me of a gem that decks
    A robe of milk-white lace.

   *   *   *   *   *

Who weaved the canopy of Night,
 And stretched it out on high ?
Who hath upheld, through ages past,
 The pillars of the sky ?

Who fixed the twinkling stars above,
 Like diamonds set in blue ?
Who caused the marshalled hosts of heav'n
 To march before my view ?

I look'd above, no answer heard,
 For stillness reigned abroad ;
But to my soul the silence said,
 " Thy Saviour is our God."

1859—1860.

FOREVERMORE.

I STROLLED along a river's side,
   When eve had chased the day away;
The first lone star had just appeared,
   The moon shone forth with soft, pale ray.
I listened to the rippling waves,
   That gently laved the pebbly shore;
I thought I heard a still, small voice,
   That murmured soft, " Forevermore !"

O mighty word ! how grand ! how vast !
   Higher than mind of man can soar ;
A thousand years have passed away,
   The future is " Forevermore !"
Our bodies die, descend to dust,
   But our immortal spirits soar
Unto the great, white Throne of God,
   To fix their fate " Forevermore !"

In robes of white, with crowns of gold,
   Bought by the suff'rings Jesus bore,
We'll reign in glory with the Lamb,
   And sing His praise " Forevermore !"
Or in the cavern of Despair,
   In anguish terrible and sore,

Confined, and bound with chains of sin,
   Forever! aye! "Forevermore!"

The lone star fixed its eye on me,
   The whisp'ring wind the question bore
To my own soul, "Art thou prepared
   To live forever—evermore?"
I answered, "Yes!" in Christ I trust,
   On Calvary all my sins he bore;
In heav'n with Him I hope to reign,
   And bless his name "Forevermore!"

HA! HA! BAY, *July*, 1858.

STONE MOUNTAIN IN MOONLIGHT.

I stood upon the mountain's brow,
  That tow'ring pile of stone;
The evening breezes round me blew,
  As I stood there—alone.
The grey clouds, riding on the winds,
  Raced swiftly o'er the sky;
Beams streaming from the lamp of Night,
  I faintly could descry.

Beneath the flying, fleecy clouds,
  The stars were hid awhile;
But, as the clouds passed by, they would
  Within the azure smile.
The silv'ry moon was veiled, but now
  Her face serene appears;
The light she sendeth forth is like
  A maiden's smile through tears.

The Rock in majesty doth rise,
  And, with a mien sublime,
It soars above the clouds, that round
  Its summit strive to climb.
The granite 'neath the moonbeams pale,
  Is silver'd with their light;

In lofty grandeur there it stands,
  A giant robed in white!

The trees, like spectral watchmen, guard
  Its lonely, barren side;
And, silent, through the leafy boughs,
  The moonbeams softly glide.
The glitt'ring raindrops on each stem
  With borrow'd radiance glow;
They shine like little stars, and thus
  Their source of light they show.

Unbroken silence reigned supreme;
  Then, standing pensive there,
I thought of Olive's lonely shade
  Where Jesus knelt in prayer.
This mountain hath, through many an age,
  The fiercest storms defied;
Thus, 'tis an emblem of the Rock—
  Christ Jesus crucified.

STONE MOUNTAIN, GEORGIA, *February*, 1859.

THE SKY AT NIGHT:

A COLLOQUY BETWEEN OBSERVATION, FANCY, AND THE SOUL.

Fancy often views an object in entirely different aspects. Fancy and Comparison behold in one thing a resemblance to many things, and discover, in the natural, the shadow of the spiritual. The one restrains and modifies the other. Fancy not only keeps Comparison from being mere matter of fact, but also imbues it with an elevated spirit—that "fine phrenzy" of which the immortal Shakspeare has written. Comparison, on the other hand, gives definiteness to Fancy; enables it to exalt the mind; transforms it into a two-edged sword for the use of the orator, and into a fountain of power for the pen of the writer. Without Comparison, Fancy would be mere Ideality, and its possession would be undesirable, for its exercise would but bewilder.

Fancy and Imagination are distinct. The former is but the play, the sparkle of the Intellect; the latter, the "faculty divine"—the spirit's vision—the power of conception—which enables a man vividly to realize an idea, or portray to himself the unseen.

Obs.—To what wilt thou compare the sky at
    night,
In which the stars appear so calmly bright,
While snow-white vapors sail the blue expanse,
And e'en the beauty of the scene enhance?

Fancy.—The veil that hides the face of Heaven
    from view,
While yet celestial brilliance shineth through;
A curtain pinned with gems of purest ray,
Behind whose shade reclines the weary Day.
God's royal robe of blue, with diamonds twined,
Is Midnight's mantle to my raptured mind;
A waveless sea, where white-winged angels glide,
Whose eyes illuminate the dark blue tide;
An emblem of existence! how sublime!
Each star a soul within the sky of Time!
A jewelled cushion for the Saviour's feet,
Enthroned forever on the Mercy Seat:
A volume bound in blue, each star a line,
That speaks a Cause omnipotent, divine:
And in the " Milky Way " where planets roll,
I see the Author of the Human Soul.

Obs.—A Cause divine? Pray is this Fancy's
    fruit?
Or is it blossom sprung from Reason's root?

Soul.—'Tis each, and both; because if God, alone
With Fancy had endowed me, she would own
His being first; but since Jehovah crowned
My Reason king, then I am surely bound,
By list'ning to myself, His power to own.
O Thou! to whom Eternity's a throne,
Omnipotence a sceptre, Truth a crown,

And Perfect Holiness a spotless gown;
Ancient of Days! deep Love and Wisdom meet,
A glorious Rainbow o'er Thy jasper seat;
Eternal Majesty enwraps Thy brow,
And Thou shalt ever be what Thou art now:
Great God! in true humility I bow,
I am, and, in my being, seen art Thou!

If Reason said, "No God," then Fancy's voice
Would cry against the mad apostate's choice,
And drive him from his madness by her voice,
But now, in God, my Father, both rejoice.

If Fancy, freed from Reason, roamed abroad,
She soon would fancy that there is a God;
For Fancy, viewing Nature's perfect laws,
Would fancy the existence of a Cause;
And when their wisdom shone before her eyes,
She would exclaim, "The First Cause must be
      wise;"
And when she knew that, since their rule began,
They have enlarged and blessed the soul of man,
And furnished him with raiment and with food,
She would declare, "The First Cause must be
      good;"
For He, in thoughtful mercy, plans has laid,
To bless the creatures whom His hand hath made.
And when she saw these wondrous laws unite,
To keep the course of mighty Nature right—

To guide a world through fields of ether blue,
And feed a blade of grass with drops of dew—
Without suspending action for an hour,
She then would own the all-pervading power,
The everlasting might of Nature's God,
And tread the path that Reason always trod.

1859–1860.

CORN IN THE BLADE.

STANZAS.

I sat upon the moonlit shore,
And listen'd to the rippling wave,
That broke upon the rocky beach,
While music rose from ev'ry lave.

How calmly beauteous was the scene,
That stretched afar before my gaze!
Like dreams the isles appeared, baptized
In star-irradiated haze.

The envious stars could not decide
Who should the queen celestial be,
So each, to view her radiant form,
Into a mirror turned the sea.

I gazed upon the spangled sky,
God's jewelled robe it seemed to me;
I looked beneath, and, lo! I saw
Its lights reflected in the sea!

The vast expanse, bestud with worlds—
God's lamps hung out from heav'n at night-
Appear'd a shoreless, surgeless sea,
Suffused with pallid, magic light.

How strangely calm! how vast the scene!
Conviction thrilled my inmost soul,
And, through my heart of hearts, a gush
Of awe and veneration stole.

"O God! Thou art, for Nature is,"
The silent stars sang in the sky;
"O God! Thou art, for Nature is,"
The heaving Ocean made reply!

1859–1860.

HYMNS.

A WISH.

The following unpretending verses were written by the author a few hours before he preached his first sermon, if a child's recommendation of Jesus might be so called, and sung, on that occasion, by the congregation. His age, at this period, was about fifteen years and three months.

A HOLY wish my heart hath bound,
To consecrate my powers to God,
Salvation's trump aloud to sound,
And preach His ever blessèd Word.

To show my Saviour on the Tree,
The thorny crown, the piercèd side,
To urge my fellow-men to flee,
And wash them in the crimson tide.

To lead repentant souls to Christ,
To hear them sing, with raptured joy,
Hosannas loud to Him who died,
To give them peace without alloy.

To guide, to strengthen, and sustain
The weak and weary by the way,
To meet them all at Jesus' feet
Upon the last, appointed day.

5

Oh ! what a glorious work is this !
Oh ! what unworthiness is mine !
But for my weakness Thou hast strength,
So all the glory shall be Thine.

1858.

HIS NAMES.

What a study the names of the Saviour, and their significant import, are for the Christian mind! When we think of the Redeemer as "Jehovah Jesus"—for Isaiah prophesied that he should be called "The Mighty God," and "The Everlasting Father"—we realize that He not only possesses all the moral attributes of the Deity, but that He is also infinite, eternal, and unchangeable. When we meditate upon Him as "Immanuel," we see Jehovah, "manifest in the flesh;" for the signification of the word is "*God with us.*" When Jesus is considered as "The Man of Sorrows," we are not only assured that He most keenly felt the pangs of grief Himself, but, also, that he now sympathizes with all His people who are in any wise afflicted.

> "In every pang that rends the heart,
> The Man of Sorrows had a part;
> He sympathizes with our grief,
> And to the suff'rer sends relief."

When we behold Jesus as the "Lamb of God"—God's sinless sacrifice for sinful man—we witness the price of our redemption; and the scenes which transpired on Calvary arise in all their terror before us. The unmitigated darkness, the vail of the Temple in twain, the heaving earth, the rending rocks, the opening graves, the fiendish multitude, the far-off disciples, the women who loved the Saviour, the eminence, the three crosses, and the one Sacrifice, appear in all their horror and mystery to our mental vision!

> " 'Tis finished! the Messiah dies
> For sins, but not His own ;
> The great redemption is complete,
> Aud Satan's power o'erthrown."

When Christ as the " Great, High Priest " who has entered within the vail, is the object of our contemplation, we remember that He once was dead, and that He is now alive forevermore. The fact that He passed through the dread, mysterious portal of death, robs the grave of its terror and gloom, and sheds around it, to us who believe, a halo of glory. We also experience the cheering assurance, that "He ever liveth to make intercession for us ;" and that, because He lives, we shall live also. "For we are dead, and our life is hid with Christ in God. When Christ, who is our life, shall appear, then shall we also appear with Him in glory."

> " As Jesus died, and rose again,
> Victorious from the dead ;
> So His disciples rise and reign
> With their triumphant Head."

Jesus is our "All in All." He is the "foundation stone," the beginning, the continuation, and the consummation of our redemption. He is the Author of our life, the Preserver of our health, the Soother of our sorrows, and the Author of every good and perfect gift. Faith in His atonement, resurrection and mediation, makes us partakers of the divine nature ; and the assurance of the possession of His love transforms our souls into fountains of celestial joy—"wells of water springing up into everlasting life." " For of Him are we in Christ Jesus, who of God is made unto us wisdom, and righteousness, and sanctification, and redemption." The Saviour is our "All in All" now, and

we will find, beyond the grave, an immortality of blessed-
ness in His presence and love.

"Jesus Christ, the same yesterday, to-day and forever!"

1860.

HIS NAMES.

Jehovah Jesus! God adored
 By seraphs in the sky,
I bow before Thy sacred throne,
 Before Thy Majesty!

Immanuel! Incarnate God,
 In Bethlehem I see!
Ye angels look! ye mortals gaze!
 How great the Mystery!

The Man of Sorrows! Nazarene,
 Whom sons of men despise;
A wand'rer on this weary earth,
 In poverty He lies!

The Lamb of God! The Sacrifice
 Suspended on the tree!
He groans, He prays, He bleeds, He dies,
 To set His people free!

The Great, High Priest, who intercedes
 For us, before the Throne;
Who ever lives to plead for those
 Who trust in Him alone!

Our All in All! we will ascribe
   Honor and praise to Thee!
Let heav'nly choirs the anthem raise
   Throughout eternity!

July, 1858.

OUR NEW YEAR'S GATHERING.

Written for, and sung by the children of the Sabbath
School connected with the North Baptist Church, in the
city of New York.

Come, children of the Sabbath School,
    Come, and an off'ring bring
Of praise sincere to Jesus' name—
    Oh! come, and sweetly sing.
Sing, for the Shepherd of the lambs
    Hath led us through the past,
With countless blessings crowned our heads,
    His arms around us cast.

Come, children, and a tribute bring
On this, our New Year's Gathering!

The Saviour came, and from our School
    Some lilies bore away,
He planted them in heav'n above,
    To blossom there—for aye.
Another year has swiftly gone,
    And, called by love divine,
Some little ones have flown away,
    In glory bright to shine.

And now in Paradise they sing,
On this, our New Year's Gathering.

The Saviour came, and to Himself
  He called, with gentle voice,
Same new-found lambs into His fold,
  They now in Him rejoice.
Their hearts are filled with Jesus' love,
  Their lips proclaim His praise;
They, to Redemption's glorious theme,
  In songs their voices raise.

And thus His wondrous love they sing,
On this, our New Year's Gathering.

For tender care, for grace bestowed,
  And loving-kindness shown
Unto this day,—with grateful hearts
  Let us surround the throne.
Oh! let us join the ransomed choir
  Of children saved above,
Who praise the Lamb on harps of gold,
  In realms of holy love!—

Oh! let us join them as they sing,
On this, our New Year's Gathering.

December, 1858.

AN ANNIVERSARY HYMN.

Written for, and sung by the children of the Sabbath School connected with the North Baptist Church in the city of New York.

Your voices, all ye children, tune,
The choral notes of love to raise ;
Let grateful incense from our hearts
In silence rise to Jesus' praise,
  For He with blessings rich and free
  Hath crowned our Anniversary.

While many children in the grave
Asleep do lie, to wake no more,
We, by the grace of God, appear
On Hope's bright side of Death's dark shore.
  Praise God ! from death we all are free,
  On this, our Anniversary.

We dwell where Freedom's planet shines,
Though millions never see its light,
And through our land the Gospel's voice
Is heard in all its saving might.
  Let " Thanks to God !" our anthem be,
  On this, our yearly Jubilee.

   5*

Among our number many feel
The power of Christ to save the soul :
In glory they shall bless His name,
While everlasting ages roll.
  " Redemption full ! Salvation free !"
  They sing, on this, our Jubilee.

For Sabbath Schools we bless the Lord,
For teachers faithful, kind, and true,
But—hark ! Some angels catch the strain,
And sweetly sing, " We join with you !"
  For they were led to Jesus here,
  And now they reign in heav'n's bright
   sphere.

Your voices, all ye children, tune,
The choral notes of love to raise ;
Friends, teachers, all, unite to sound
A joyful song to Jesus' praise !
  Oh ! may it thus in glory be
  Our joy to hold a Jubilee !

June, 1859.

EVENTFUL MOMENTS.

Nothing but a vital faith in a living Saviour, a faith which manifests itself in uniting our souls to God, and in the constant performance of Christ-like actions, can prepare us fearlessly to meet the dread realities of Death, Judgment, and Eternity. Is this faith yours?

EVENTFUL moment! when our friends,
    Stand, sad and breathless, nigh,
And gaze with tearful eyes, to view
    Their fellow-mortal die!

Eventful moment! when the wave
    Of life breaks on the shore
Of vast Eternity, whose coast
    The mind fails to explore!

Eventful moment ! when the mist
    Of time begins to fly,
And great realities unfold
    Before the spirit's eye!

Eventful moment! when the throne
    Of God appears in sight,
Unto a soul emerging from
    The gloom of earthly night!

When glorious heaven and dreadful hell
   Are viewed by one, who knows
That he must dwell eternally
   In endless joys or woes!

Eventful moment! when the voice
   Of God to Judgment calls;
When Death, obedient, breaks the chain
   Which deathless being thralls!

O Jesus! teach me how to die,
   Bestow the gift of faith,
Which robs the grave of all its power,
   And triumphs over Death!

Then, O my soul! Death will unite
   Thee to thy living Head;
And ope the gate of Paradise
   Where Death himself is dead!

September, 1859.

THE VISION OF JOHN.

A PARAPHRASE.

See the 21st and 22d Chapters of Revelation.

I, JOHN, a servant of the Lord,
In Patmos' lonely isle was bound;
But Christ was there, and in His love
Deep joy in banishment I found.

He sent an Angel to reveal
The glories of the upper sphere,
Where countless hosts, like radiant stars,
Throughout immensity appear.

I saw Jerusalem descend,
God's glory round the city shone
Bright as a diamond in the sun;
Her light was like a jasper-stone.

I then beheld twelve pearly gates—
Twelve Angel-watchmen standing there;
How clear the wall's foundations were!
The silver Moon's not half so fair!

The wall was built of jasper-stone,
O'er its bright surface Seraphs trod;

And streets of burnished gold adorned
   The glorious city of my God.

No gorgeous temple met my gaze ;
   Where veiléd Seraphim bow low
Before the Throne, I only saw
   A spotless Lamb, as white as snow.

He was their temple—at His shrine
   Were kneeling nations bathed in light ;
And kings before Him prostrate fell,
   They owned His gentleness and might.*

A river clear as crystal flowed
   From out the great white Throne of God,
And rippling through the golden streets,
   Its murmuring music sent abroad.

The branches of the Tree of Life
   Drooped o'er the peaceful, limpid stream,
While, hanging in celestial light,
   The fruit in loveliness did gleam.

And those who taste the leaves that wave
   Above Life's river, shall be healed ;
The curse of sin these leaves destroy :
   This blessed truth the Lord hath sealed !

* Gentleness as the "Lamb of God," and "Might," as the
victorious Saviour.

The saints who dwell in Paradise
   No candle need, or shining sun;
For in the light of Jesus' love
   A brighter glory they have won.

That glory, like that glory's Source,
   Can never, never fade away;
The hosts who see His face, behold
   The sun of an eternal day!

"O glorious truth!" the Angel cried,
   "These sayings faithful are and true;
For I am sent these things to show
   To God's elect, by showing you!"

Then adoration filled my soul,
   Before the Angel's feet I fell,
And would have worshipp'd, but he said,
   "Arise, arise, thou dost not well!

"For I thy fellow-servant am,
   The prophet's pathway I have trod,
And kept the sayings of this book:
   My brother, rise and WORSHIP GOD!"

September, 1859.

A WONDER.

When we meditate on the depravity of our state by nature, and then remember that we now love Jesus, *because He first loved us*, we are lost in amazement. The grace of God, as it has been, and is still manifested toward us, is entirely unaccountable. No reason can be submitted *why* the Son of God felt such a degree of love for a sinful world as to be constrained to die for its redemption. The most gigantic intellects, angels, and archangels, cannot solve the problem.

While a believer rejoices in the assurance that the love of Jesus is exercised toward him, at the same time he wonders why it should be so. Confessing his inability to solve the mystery, he is ready to say of the Saviour's love what Job said of the nature of God: "It is higher than heaven; what can I do? It is deeper than hell; what can can I know?" Why, that the mountains shall depart, and the hills remove, but His love shall never fail, nor be withdrawn from thee; for "the measure thereof is longer than the earth, and broader than the sea."

The Son of God loved me, and gave himself for me.— PAUL.

O WONDROUS truth! the Saviour loves
   A sinful worm like me,
While angels bright surround His Throne,
   From sin's pollution free!
Surpassing strange that Heav'nly Love
   Should fold His wings o'er me,

When Seraphs, clothed in robes of white,
　Before Him bend the knee !

Yet stranger far, that Christ should leave
　His glorious throne above,
And on our sinful world appear,
　To show His wondrous love ;
That heav'n's great king and Sovereign Lord,
　The Ruler of the sky,
Should come in human form to earth,
　And in a manger lie !

Despised among the sons of men,
　"The Man of Sorrows" He ;
His heart with grief acquaintance made,
　Because He lovéd me.
My sins did pierce Immanuel's side,
　They nailed Him to the tree ;
He wore a crown of twisted thorns,
　Because He lovéd me.

O wondrous love ! transcendant grace !
　How full ! how vast ! how free !
Behold the amazing sacrifice,
　He gave Himself for me !
While everlasting ages roll,
　My God, I will praise Thee ;
And, oh ! the story of Thy Love
　Will fill eternity.

December, 1858.

THE WORLD'S ANTHEM.

Though the world is influenced by Satan, it is yet the property of God, and as the purifying influence of the Gospel is extended, it will manifest clearer and more beautiful evidences of its Possessor's nature.

FROM ev'ry clime, in various tongues,
 A universal choir
Harmonious sound the praise of God,
 And souls with joy inspire.

Salvation's song from Albion's shores
 Is heard across the sea ;
And strains from Ireland's isle arise,
 A glorious jubilee !

Sweet notes of love from Sweden's hills,
 Are wafted on the breeze ;
And sons of Tell an anthem raise,
 That soundeth o'er the seas.

Low whisperings from sable breasts,
 Arise to God's right hand ;
For Christ rejoices when he hears
 A note from Afric's strand !

A joyful song ascends to-day,
  From rich, poor, bond, and free,
Who, on Columbia's shores, exult
  In Gospel liberty.

Soon may the period come, (O earth,
  Roll quickly round the sun !)
When all, who feel the Gospel's power,
  Shall be, in Jesus, one !

From ransom'd souls on China's fields,
  Salvation's song hath risen ;
May China, glorious, soon emerge
  From superstition's prison !

These anthems mingle with the shout
  From India's sunny plains,
Where swarthy sons of earth exult,
  Because the Saviour reigns.

The angels hear the music of
  The universal choir,
Then, simultaneous, strike their harps,
  And worlds with joy inspire !

November, 1859.

TO THE MISSIONARY.

The life of a devoted Missionary is one of the truest manifestations of the spirit of Jesus. The blessed Saviour left the delights and glories of heaven on a mission of mercy, prompted by love for a ruined world. The Christian Missionary, constrained by the same spirit, forsakes his country, friends, and home, and departs to bear the glad tidings of salvation to those who sit in the darkness of heathenism. If we had existed and loved the Saviour when He was on earth, would we not have supplied His every want? Would He ever have suffered from hunger, thirst, and exposure, if we had possessed a crust, a cup of water, and a hut? Never! The Missionary is, in a peculiar sense, the representative of Christ, and shall we, who love the precious Saviour, ever allow His peculiar representatives to suffer anxiety on account of the wants of themselves and their families? No! we will provide for them, as we would have provided for Jesus. Oh! that this were the language of Christendom!

Thou herald of the Cross, arise,
　And leave thy native shore;
The Saviour left His Father's breast,
　A cross for thee He bore.
Exalt a dying, risen Christ,
　For sinners slain and raised,
Till, by a dark, benighted soul,
　His wondrous love is praised;

Till songs from countless multitudes
   Of ransomed ones ascend,
Till ev'ry knee, at Jesus' name,
   In penitence shall bend ;
Till angels swell the choral notes,
   Till heav'n's high arches ring,
Because the distant isles have crowned
   Christ Jesus Lord and King.

*   *   *   *   *   *   *

Fear not, thou servant of the Lord,
   Oh ! never be dismayed ;
Should He who standeth on the Rock
   Of Ages be afraid ?
Thy heart should never know a fear,
   Or dread an evil day,
Since Jesus to thy soul hath said,
   " I am with thee alway."

Then faint not, soldier of the Cross,
   The Captain's near thy side,
To guide and cheer, defend and bless ;
   No evil can betide.
Oh ! falter not ! The great reward
   Is worthy of the pain :
The bitter cross must first be borne,
   The glorious crown to gain.

Thy crown is souls redeemed from sin,
　　Each soul a gem of light,
Whose value far exceeds the stars
　　That glitter in the night.
Oh! what a glorious crown to cast
　　Before the Saviour's feet,
When, in the Paradise of God,
　　Our Saviour thou shalt meet.

February, 1859.

AN APPEAL.

The sympathies of Jesus were universal. Degradation in all its forms, and woe in every aspect, moved His tender heart. He never restrained His feelings, but allowed them to prompt Him to action. "Though he was rich, yet for our sakes He became poor, that we through his poverty might be made rich. "He appeared on earth, the divine, martyr Missionary, accomplished His work, sealed his testimony, and consummated the plan of Redemption by the shedding of His blood. The Gospel which He proclaimed, the only means by which the world can be regenerated, has been committed to our care. Shall, we by sinful indifference, limit its redeeming influence, and thereby strengthen the kingdom of Satan? God forbid! Let us remember and succor the millions that lie in the darkness of superstition, awaiting the dawn of divine truth. Let us bear the Gospel to the heathen ourselves, or send, or help to send, a Missionary in our place.

> "Ye who the name of Jesus hear,
>   His sacred steps pursue,
> And let the mind which was in Him
>   Be also found in you."

I HEAR a voice from heathen lands,
The Macedonian cry comes o'er
The bosom of the heaving sea,
And soundeth on Columbia's shore.

It tells of darkness, Stygian gloom,
Which everlasting being shrouds,
Of superstition's blinding veil,
Which wraps the Deity in clouds.

It speaks of souls, undying souls,
Descending swiftly down to hell,
While in the Paradise of God
A host of ransomed spirits dwell :
While Jesus left us this command,
" My wondrous love proclaim to all,
Glad tidings preach to ev'ry soul,
Who breathes on this terrestrial ball."

Awake! ye ransomed of the Lord!
Arise! Arise! in Jesus' name,
And consecrate your prayers and wealth,
His blessed Gospel to proclaim!
Uphold the Missionary's hands,
Inspire, by acts of love, his heart,
Inflame his soul with Christ-like zeal,
By bearing, each and all, your part.

But leave him not alone, to pine
For sympathy, for prayers, and bread,
Lest God in dreadful vengeance hurl
His curses on your guilty head ;
Lest all the angels weeping stand,
In silent, infinite surprise ;

Lest ev'ry harp in heav'n be hushed,
And boundless wonder fill the skies;

Lest anguish thrill again the heart
Of Him, who, for our ransom, died;
And He, in agony, repent
That ever He was crucified!
Awake! Awake! O Church of God!
The Gospel's trailing banner raise,
And let it wave o'er ev'ry land,
Till earth resounds with Jesus' praise.

1859–1860.

JOY IN SORROW

LIFE IN DEATH.

THE SEPARATION.

The incident, which prompted the following lines, tran-
spired in the Spring of 1859, when the Georgia Baptist
Convention, which had convened in the beautiful city of
Columbus, and enjoyed a blessed session, was broken up.

THE aged saints of God had met in peace,
And in His holy house, with prayer and praise,
Rejoiced.   And in communion sweet
Around the fireside, at the twilight hour,
And in the evening, underneath the shade
Of trees, that rise below the Southern moon,
They had refreshed their souls.   But now they
    stand,
An ancient group, within the sacred walls.
The parting hour has come, and ev'ry heart
Yields gently to its sad, soul-moving sway.
They grieve and hope in perfect unison,
And seek and find the Saviour's sympathy.
They feel the need of faith, they realize
Its power ; and ere they separate, they pray.

A hoary-headed saint, whose calm blue eyes
Shone with an earnest light through falling tears,
Before the Throne of Grace, upon his knees,
In adoration bowed ; and, spreading out his
    hands,

And lifting up his weeping eyes to heav'n,
He, in a voice of awe, deep, thrilling, low,
Communed and pleaded with the Deity.
And, while his soul arose, the silent prayers
Of all around were wafted to the Throne ;
And Jesus, as they rose, inhaled them there,
And, pure, He breathed them out to God, who sat
Upon a universal Mercy-seat,
And, smiling, hailed His well-beloved Son !

The answer came as struggling sunshine falls
Upon an April day, till Nature smiles,
And all her raindrop-tears, like jewels, shine.
The aged saints arose.   Their faces shone
Like Moses' on the Mount; victorious faith
And Christian love, spoke through their earnest
    eyes—
The mirrors of the human soul, by which
The silent spirit eloquently speaks.

They now must part.   Oh ! shall they ever kneel
Together round the Throne of Grace again ?
Shall their united voices ever rise
From earth once more ?   Before a year has
    passed,
Shall not a form familiar lie asleep
Within the tomb ?   They stood, and sadly
    gazed,

With speaking eyes, on one another's face ;
They gazed, till coursing down their wrinkled
    cheeks,
The tear-drops fell. The strong men wept aloud,
For neither faith nor love could take away
The grief of parting from their swelling hearts.
Yea, in the fullness of that sacred hour,
They threw their arms around each other's neck,
And sobbed a last farewell. " Farewell," they
    said,
Then sad and silently, they turned away.

*   *   *   *   *   *   *

O three times blesséd thought! In Paradise
They shall united be, to part no more.
Then from their eyes the Lord shall wipe away
The tears of woe ; then Jesus' smile shall dry
The marks of grief ; then shall their hoary hairs
Be changéd into bright, immortal crowns.
Their eyes shall beam with everlasting joy ;
Their bodies like to Christ's shall be transformed ;
Arrayed in spotless white they shall appear ;
And, holding in their hands their harps of gold,
Shall praise the Lamb of God forevermore !

1859.

LINES ON THE DEATH OF A PASTOR.

Rev. A. Kingman Nott, the young and talented pastor of the First Baptist Church in this city, passed into the land of the living on July 7th, 1859. We who remain, are yet in the land of the dying.

The departed was greatly and justly beloved. Though flattered on every hand, his deportment was unassuming, and truly humble. His countenance was the index of his soul, and its expression spoke of gentleness and amiability. He had a kind word and look for all, and, consequently, won the affection of every honest heart.

As a pastor he was eminently successful. If ever a young servant of Christ had bright prospects of future usefulness, well-founded hopes of being instrumental in the upbuilding of our Redeemer's cause, it was the departed.

At the time of his decease he was only twenty-five years of age. How young to die! How strange that God should have taken him away! If an aged warrior had fallen, we would not have wondered, but when a Christian soldier, young, energetic and brave, is removed, we think the dealings of Providence mysterious.

DEDICATED TO THE MEMBERS OF THE FIRST BAPTIST CHURCH.

JEHOVAH's path is girt with clouds,
   And deepest darkness shrouds His throne;
The thoughts, the plans, and purposes
   Of God, are known to God alone.

Yet, though the darkness mocks our gaze,
   And veils the path we seek to trace,
We know, that angel Mercy flies,
   With radiant wings, before His face.

To Calvary's Cross the Angel points,
   Where Jesus died to save His sheep;
And, looking down, she drops a tear,
   To see the flocks bereaved that weep.
Then, mourners, fear not, Mercy pleads,
   Compassion dims her weeping eye ;
If Christ is love, and Christ your friend,
   Have faith, Himself He'll not deny.

Beloved in Christ, your hearts are sad,
   Your pastor's sleeping in the grave;
Yet, murmur not, but humbly say
   "God taketh only what He gave."
Ye sorrow o'er his lifeless corse,
   Ye weep, for dust to dust is given ;
But let your souls in hope rejoice,
   His ransomed spirit's safe in heaven.

The hallowed pulpit's vacant now,
   Where oft his head was bowed in prayer;
The very loneliness proclaims
   To ev'ry heart, "*He is not there.*"
His peaceful eye, his noble brow,
   His youthful form lie cold and low ;

6*

And weeping Faith can scarce confess,
"*'Tis better that it should be so.*"

His voice within the old church walls,
   The Sabbath silence breaks no more ;
And Sorrow broods with folded wings,
   Where Hope exultant reigned before.
And yet no grief, no sense of joy,
   No ease, without first anxious care ;
No death, no life beyond the grave,
   No parting here, no meeting there.

Among the blood-washed throng, by faith,
   Your pastor, near the Throne, I see,
And, in a glorious halo wrapt,
   *A hoary head appears to me !**
Wait, toil, and pray till Jesus calls,
   And then upon the heav'nly shore,
You'll meet the pastor of your hearts,
   With all the loved ones gone before.

1859–1860.

* An allusion to the sainted Cone, who was pastor of the First Church, previously to Mr. Nott.

THE LITTLE MAIDEN.

I LOVED a little maiden, I thought that she loved
    me,
I thought I saw love beaming through her bon-
    nie, dark blue e'e ;
I thought I heard love whisper in the tremor of
    her voice,
Like sighing summer breezes, that make the
    woods rejoice.

I loved a little maiden so deeply and so free,
But love no longer beameth through her bonnie,
    dark blue e'e,
To me and earth it's glassy, and it will not shine
    again,
The maiden has departed from earth, and sin and
    pain.

The little maiden's body lies 'neath a shady tree,
Where faintly sounds the murmur of the rolling,
    deep, blue sea,
In calmest nights I wander there when moon-
    shine's on the lea,
The stars bring to remembrance the beaming of
    her e'e.

The little maiden's spirit rests in sereneness now,
Her eye, with peace, is beauteous, and unshaded
    is her brow,
Her voice, so low and silv'ry, maketh music in
    the sky,
The little maiden liveth, though dead, she did
    not die.

Of her fair robe the pureness vies with her bosom
    white,
Her angel-form is gliding throughout the fields
    of light,
And beams of heav'nly beauty illume her holy
    face,
The beams are light reflected from Christ the
    King of grace.

A never fading garland entwines her snow-white
    brow,
She standeth in His presence before whom angels
    bow ;
I look through heaven's windows—the twinkling
    stars of night—
To me the maid appeareth, crowned, beautiful,
    and white.

April, 1859.

LOVE TESTED.

It matters not how deeply we love, we are sure to realize the extent of our affection more vividly when separated. Perhaps the cause of this is, that we are unable so fully to manifest our love when apart, as when united. However this may be, we know that death will test the nature of all our attachments, and nothing, save the belief in a future state of happy reunion, can fill the void caused by the removal of one, much beloved, and fondly cherished. How supremely should we love our Lord and Saviour Jesus Christ, "who hath abolished death, and brought life and immortality to light through the Gospel!"

We know we love when we imprint
  A kiss upon the loved one's cheek,
And see the dark, uplifted eye
  Of passion and affection speak.

We almost know how *much* we love,
  When from our loved one forced to part;
For then the tendrils stretch that bind
  The loved one closely to our heart.

We *think* we know how much we love,
  When, kneeling by the loved one's side,
We watch, with unbelieving eyes, .
  The ebbing of existence' tide.

We *say* we know how much we love,
   When gazing, tearless, on the form
Bereft of life and thought by death,
   As trees of blossoms by a storm.

We *never* know how much we love,
   Till standing, weeping, near a tomb,
We see the lifeless form consigned
   To dust, oblivion and gloom.

For, ah! in that sad moment we
   Forget the form is only clay,
And that the spirit never knows
   Annihilation or decay.

There is a land, afflicted soul,
   Where hearts by grief are never riven ;
" Good-bye !" or " Dead !" is heard no more,
   That land, afflicted soul, is heaven !

Then, oh! when sorrow clouds thy brow,
   And agonizing is thy heart,
Think of the land where angels sing,
   " We love, but never, never part !"

March, 1860.

TO A DYING ORPHAN.

Thou art passing, gentle Annie,
    From the vale of tears,
Watered by the stream of sorrow,
    Shaded by our fears,
To the land of fadeless glory,
    Where no clouds arise
Along the infinite expanse,
    Darkening its skies.

Thou art passing, patient Annie,
    From thy couch of pain,
To the land where weary mortals
    Never sigh again;
Where no sick ones ever languish
    Through the night or day,
For sin and death from Life's domain
    Banished are, for aye.

Thy cheek that bloomed is pale, Annie,
    Snow-white is thy brow;
From thine eyes the light is fading,
    Death is near thee now.
Like a star that disappeareth
    In the distant west,
Thou art passing, calm and peaceful,
    To eternal rest.

Thou art passing, dying Annie,
    From thy friends below ;
They are mourning round thee, Annie,
    Sobbing in their woe ;
While thy father and thy mother,
    On the heav'nly shore,
Wait thy coming, there they'll call thee
    " Orphan girl " no more.

When thou ent'rest Death's dark valley,
    Christ shall give thee light,
Glory's gate unto thy spirit
    Shall be Death's dark night.
He who died and rose triumphant,
    Shall disperse the gloom ;
On the mystic way to glory,
    Lead thee through the tomb.

Clothed in robes of snowy whiteness,
    There shalt thou appear,
And thine eyes, beholding Jesus,
    Never shed a tear.
There the Lamb shall lead thee, Annie,
    Through the pastures green,
By the river, clear as crystal,
    Eye hath never seen.

*   *   *   *   *

LIFE IN DEATH.

The moon shines o'er thy grave, Annie,
    Evening breezes sigh
Through the little, quiet churchyard,
    Where the dead ones lie.
There I strolled when falling shadows
    Mantled earth in gloom,
When, from boundless ether, planets
    Twinkled o'er thy tomb.

And I sadly muséd, Annie,
    On the visions bright,
Fancy painted in thy future,
    Shrouded now in night.
Knelt I weeping in the churchyard,
    On the dewy sod ;
Angels whispered—" Annie resteth
    On the breast of God."

1859–1860.

THE DEATH OF SISTER MARY.

TO H. C.

As a murm'ring, sun-lit ripple
   Breaks upon the white sea-sand,
Broke the life-wave of my sister
   On this shaded, earthly strand.

As a star that gently fadeth
   From its station in the sky
When the light of morning dawneth,
   So did darling Mary die.

As the sun reclines in slumber
   On the bosom of the sea,
Traces of his beauty leaving,
   Which proclaim he yet shall be;

So my gentle, blue-eyed sister
   Faded from the shore of Time—
Passed serenely through the gateway
   Of Eternity sublime.

When the wings of Death's dark angel
   On her brow a shadow threw,

Jesus' love her face illumined,
 And the shade of Death withdrew.

Patient, little Mary waited
 Calm and peaceful to the last,
Then a cloud of glory veiled her,
 Smiling into heav'n she passed.

Rest thee! rest thee! darling sister,
 On thy Saviour's bosom rest!
Hush, thou wounded heart, thy mourning,
 Mary is forever blest!

June, 1859.

IS SISTER MARY DEAD?

Judging from observation, one would readily imagine, that many who profess to believe the doctrines of Christianity, regard death as something nearly equivalent to annihilation. We hear bitter lamentations over husbands and wives, parents and children, lovers and friends, said to be in the grave, when nothing, save their mortal remains, the dust which the deathless spirits left behind them, is in reality there. Death only ushers us into a different state of existence, the great characteristic of which, is its absolute spiritualness. Our loved ones, who have passed from earth, are still alive, and that in a truer and more comprehensive sense. If they trusted in the Son of God, they not only exist, but are supremely blessed in the enjoyment of a glorious immortality.

For I am in a strait betwixt two, having a desire to depart, and to be with Christ, which is far better.—PAUL.

Jesus said unto Martha, I am the Resurrection and the Life, he that believeth in me, though he were dead, yet shall he live. And whosoever liveth and believeth in me, SHALL NEVER DIE. Believest thou this?—JOHN.

Thy voice is hushed—the lovely voice,
That laughed so joyously and free,
Is hushed, my Mary, in the grave,
It never more will gladden me.

Thine eye is dim—that sparkling eye,
So bright, so beautiful and fair,
Is cold and glassy now in death,
No loving light for me shines there.

They laid thee in thy narrow bed,
Thy bed beneath the cold, damp ground:
I sought thee in thy little grave,
Thy dust, not Mary, there was found!

I drew aside the veil that hangs
Between us and the spirit-land;
I gazed into the upper world,
And saw thee shining on its strand!

Thy robe was white, and on thy head,
There shone a glorious crown of gold;
Thine eye, once dim, was full of light,
For Jesus then thou didst behold!

And in thy hands I saw a harp,
Whence sounded music sweet and calm;
I heard the voice I loved on earth,
Ascribing praises to the Lamb!

Within the portals of the tomb,
Thy body motionless may lie;
And yet my Mary *is not dead*,
She who believes *can never die!*

Sister, farewell! thou art not lost,
Ah, no! but only gone before!
Wait for thy brother till he comes,
To meet thee on the " shining shore !"

December, 1858.

BROTHER CHARLEY.

If there were no other text in the Bible having reference to the minuteness and extent of our knowledge in the future, the following, alone, is sufficient to convince us, that we shall recognize those with whom we have associated on earth. Paul said of himself, "Now I know in part; but then I shall know even as also *I am known*." If the Apostle meant us to understand, as he doubtless did, that he would know, *as he then was known to God;* and if we may expect to possess this knowledge with the Apostle, how can we for a moment suppose that there will be no recognition in heaven? If such were the case, would we then know as we are known?

They who believe in no future recognition, urge, that if we recognize friends in heaven, we will also lament those who fail to reach that blessed place. In answer to this, we inquire, will a glorified saint feel, that the soul, which has deliberately sinned, during the whole period of its probation, against his Saviour, is, because of a relation once sustained in the flesh, bound to him forever by the ties of friendship? The enemies of Christ, though now related to Christians, are not their truest friends. But how much less after every earthly connection has been dissolved. "For in the resurrection they neither marry, nor are given in marriage, but are as the angels of God in heaven."

THE loved one of my heart is gone,
　　The noble and the brave;
And now the flowing tears fall fast
　　Upon my brother's grave.

They laid thee in the burial ground,
 To slumber all alone;
I often seek thy grave, but oh!
 My brother, thou art gone!

I sometimes hear thy voice in dreams,
 Speak of the realms above;
And whisper to my drooping soul,
 Of peace, and joy, and love.

I would not draw thee back to earth,
 For thou'rt supremely blest;
I would not call thee from the land,
 Where all the weary rest.

Thou mayst not leave thy heav'nly home,
 And come again to me;
But, brother, when the Saviour calls,
 I will inquire for thee.

When I approach the pearly gates,
 From death and sin set free,
I'll gaze among the white-robed throng,
 To catch a glimpse of thee!

When angels from the earth return
 With songs of jubilee;
When all the ransomed shout for joy,
 O brother! look for me!

1858–1859.

A CHILD'S VOYAGE TO HEAVEN.

AN ALLEGORY.

The " tiny vessel " is the soul of the child, and the " mystic sea " is the life of which he is scarcely conscious. The " sun of Life's fair morn " is the child's delightful assurance of existence, and the " breezes " are joys, the influence of which he feels. The " snowy sails " are the principles of his soul, which are supposed to be acted upon by joys, as sails are affected by the winds. The " heav'nly vision," is the glimpses of Paradise which are found in Revelation, and " the winds," and " wild waves," are sorrows, fears, and temptations. The remainder of the similes will be easily understood.

A TINY vessel sailed upon a mystic sea,
She just had left the port of dreaming Infancy ;
The gale of Time exhaled its unresisted breath,
To waft the little ship toward the Straits of
     Death.

The sun of Life's fair morn shone brightly on the
     sea,
The breezes rode the waves, that swelled and
     rippled free,
They filled the snowy sails, that bore the ship
     along,

They fanned the sailor's brow, and cnanted him
    a song.
He was a thoughtful boy, who just had learned
    to know,
That Life's deep waters ebb, as surely as they flow,
That he was born to live, to think, to act, to die,
And that his course was watched by God's all-
    seeing eye.

He knew the guilt of sin, which is the cause of
    Hell,
Of Paradise he'd dreamed, where holy beings
    dwell ;
He knew his ship must clear the dismal Straits
    of Death,
And thither swiftly sailed, while he inhaled his
    breath.

A heav'nly vision oft arose before his sight,
Beyond the Grave it shone, e'en in the distance,
    bright ;
The scene of beauty spoke—of glory all un-
    told—
A halo o'er the sea it cast, like burnished gold.

The sailor saw the light ! He turned his vessel's
    bow,
And steered toward the land, that seemed so dis-
    tant now ;

7

His ship was off the coast of Pleasure's danger-
ous shore,
And when her course was changed, the winds
her white sails tore.

But when the wild waves raged, and tossed his
tiny ship
Upon the foaming surge, he let the anchor slip;
The anchor's name was Faith, it grappled to a
Rock;
The vessel rode secure, and braved the tempest's
shock.

The voice of Jesus Christ appeased the troubled
tide,
And caused the little bark in peacefulness to
glide
Upon a rippling sea, till shadows o'er it hung,
And ev'ry breeze that blew, a mournful requiem
sung.

The sun of Life's fair morn was shaded by a
cloud,
Before noon's glory shone, 'twas hidden in a
shroud;
Say! Was the sun of Life to gloom eternal
given?
No! no! on earth it set, and, shadeless, rose in
Heaven!

The white sails grew obscure amidst the massive
    cloud,
That wrapped the Straits within a dark, ethereal
    shroud ;
The sailor and the ship were lost to mortal sight,
Enveloped in the gloom of an Egyptian night.

But soon the Straits were cleared, and then a
    waveless sea,
The boundless, blue expanse of vast Eternity
Was entered by the pass, named " Joy Forever-
    more,"
And there the ship was moored by the Elysian
    shore.

September, 1859.

MEMORY AND FAITH.

Memory links us to the past, and Faith to the future.
The exercise of Memory is generally sorrowful, for joy is
rarely predominant in a human life.　Memory unveils the
darker side of the Christian's immortality—leads him
through a shadowy graveyard in which his carefully-
matured plans, joyful anticipations, fondly cherished hopes,
and dearest friends, all alike blasted by the breath of Time,
have been buried, lamented, and almost forgotten.　Faith
reveals the glorious and abiding realities of the Christian's
future—links him to God through a union with Christ, and,
by the prospect and assurance of Heaven, produces within
his breast a spiritual "well of water springing up into
everlasting life."

WHILE Memory explored the Past
　　With an observant eye,
A smile suffused her face, as light
　　Illumes the evening sky;
For in her childhood's home she stood,
　　In which her youthful hours
Had blessed the early morn of life,
　　As dew-drops bless the flowers.

But sorrow darken'd Mem'ry's brow,
　　As near a grave she stood,
The little grave where brother slept,
　　Beneath the shady wood.

She plucked a rosebud from the place,
    And sadly turned away,
While, for a happier scene than this,
    She silently did pray.

But, as she turned, her glances fell
    Upon a grassy mound,
And she, in search of joyful scenes,
    A mother's tombstone found.
Poor Mem'ry wept, and madly wished
    She never had been born,
And, in her agony, she sobbed,
    " I live, and love, and mourn."

Faith heard the plaint; in Mem'ry's ear
    She whispered—" Earthly woe
Is God's dark robe; His blest designs
    Hereafter thou shalt know."
She drew aside the veil of sense,
    And showed the Land of Rest,
Where sorrow-burdened souls repose
    In peace, forever blest.

Where broken hearts by Christ are healed,
    Where tear-drops fall no more,
Where grassy mounds are never raised,
    As in the days of yore;
Where life, and love, and peace, and j'
    Supreme, eternal reign,

And from the Christian's Paradise
　　Forever banish pain.

Where spirits love eternally,
　　And know as they are known,
Where all are rich beyond degree,
　　For each calls Christ his own.
Faith fondly looked in Mem'ry's eyes,
　　The tears were gone, she smiled;
A glimpse of heav'n, to earthly woe
　　Had fully reconciled.

1859–1860.

PIECES OF SENTIMENT.

MY MOTHER'S LOVE.

When we remember, in the hour of temptation, the pious counsel of a departed mother, we may be assured that we are the objects of God's restraining grace.

My mother's love ! its hallowed power
    Hath been the day-star of my life ;
Its influence hath drawn me oft
    Away from scenes with danger rife.

When Pleasure's luring whispers fell,
    In winning accents, on my ear,
Inviting me to taste her joys,
    Without a single thought of fear,

The counsel that my mother gave,
    When I, a child, knelt by her knee,
And looked into her loving eyes,
    Came o'er the past again to me ;

And in that hour I felt her hand
    Laid, as of yore, upon my head,
I heard her voice again, and, lost
    Awhile, forgot that she was dead !

When from this reverie I waked,
    How Pleasure's painted face had changed !
7*

The scene I viewed in Mem'ry's hall,
From Pleasure had my soul estranged.

To guide the lonely orphan's feet
Where peace and glory meet above,
The angels woke within his soul
The mem'ry of his mother's love!

September, 1859.

A HOME SCENE.

'Tis Sabbath afternoon, and silver light
Is gently streaming through the window shades.
A shining beam upon the carpet sleeps,
Another woos a bunch of waxen flowers,
As if they were the handiwork of God.
Upon the portrait of a lovely girl,
With holy face, and dark, uplifted orbs,
A radiant sunbeam rests.
               The solemn clock
Ticks on the mantel ; ever and anon
I hear the rustling leaves that Mary reads,
While faintly sound the footstep and the voice
Of passers by. A sacred hush pervades
The parlor, and its power I deeply feel.
In such a hallowed hour, on Mem'ry's breast
My soul reclines, and dreams the time away.
With mellowed radiance the room's suffused,
And ev'ry one is silent.
              Mother sits
Where father often sat before he died.
Her face is sad, and yet the peace of God,
That passeth understanding, sleepeth in
The liquid depths of her dark, gentle eyes.
A panorama of the pregnant Past
Before her mental vision doth appear.

None see what mother vieweth now, because
No eye, except the eye of God, can gaze
Within the sanctuary of the soul.

The spirit's vision hath unbounded range.
Though mountains rise and oceans roll between
Us and the forms familiar to the scenes
Of childhood's days, now absent many a year,
We only need to close our eyes, and, lo !
The scenes and forms are witnessed by the soul.

A burial-place, an ivy-covered church,
An open'd gate, a silent throng that moves
Along a shaded path, a new-made grave,
Three weeping children, and a rev'rend form,
With hoary locks, calm eyes, and lofty brow,
Before my mother's spirit-vision pass.
She sees her orphans as they, wond'ring, gazed
Into their father's and her husband's grave.

A dark'ning shade upon her count'nance falls,
She heaves a deep-drawn sigh, and, lo ! a tear
Upon her silken eyelash hangs.
                              Behold
Her face.   She hears again the voice of him
Who stood beside her husband's tomb, and said,
" Fear not, lone widow, for thy Maker is
Thy Husband, and His name ' The Lord of Hosts ;'
He is the Father of the fatherless :

And, though the mountains should depart, and
    hills
Remove, yet from thee and thine orphan babes,
His loving-kindness never shall withdraw."

Her eye upon her happy children fell,
And then a gush of gratitude, too deep
For words, rose from the altar of her heart
To God, her faithful, cov'nant-keeping God.

O Memory! thou hast a magic power.

The beams that wooed the waxen flowers, and
    kissed
The portrait of the lovely girl, and slept
Upon the parlor floor, have disappeared.
Night mounts her starry throne, while shadows
    fall
Upon the earth, and Darkness wipeth out,
With silent brush, the shining tracks of Day.
The shades of gloom glide everywhere, and if
The fire emitted not a ruddy light,
Our parlor would be like the soul of man
Without the Gospel, for the curtains keep
The light of moon and stars from shining in.

February, 1860.

MUSIC.

My soul's a wondrous harp, and Music thrills,
With vivifying touches, ev'ry chord,
Until my being breathes in ecstasy,
And I, enraptured, live in melody.
And then my spirit struggles to be free,
And soar to heav'n whose air is harmony.

1860.

WHAT SHOULD I LOVE?

How strange it is that men and women, who seem to possess common sense, are so frequently captivated by the beauty that perishes! And how inexplicable that we so often fail to discover and appreciate, because concealed beneath a homely exterior, the loveliness of soul which never dies! Though beauty be only skin-deep, yet we are fascinated by it, and though there is a loveliness of mind which is immortal, still we often allow it to exercise an unappreciated and unnoticed influence.

"A woman that feareth the Lord, she shall be praised."
—Solomon.

WHAT should I love? A pretty face?
   A laughing, sparkling eye?
A winning smile? A graceful form?
   Ah, no! they all must die.

Or should I look for gleams of wit,
   That dazzle where they shine?
Alluring Beauty! should I kneel
   In homage at thy shrine?

Nay! Something nobler I demand;
   True majesty of mind,
A soul inspired with Godlike aims,
   I seek, and hope to find.

For gleams of wit, like transient life,
   In death's gloom fade away;
And beauty, like a cherished hope,
   Is blighted in a day.

A woman's soul transformed by grace,
   Devoted, changeless, true;
A woman's heart so pure that it
   Guile's shadow never knew,

I'd with my own unite in bands
   Immortal as my soul;
For when love's tide by death was stemmed,
   'Twould rise in heav'n to roll.

May, 1859.

THE CHRISTIAN LOVER'S LAY.

The exercise of love for the Saviour purifies the affection of two sympathetic hearts, and renders it, like the grand centre to which they are drawn thereby, unchangeable and immortal.

My darling, Jesus loves thee,
Oh! in His bosom rest;
Cast all thy care upon Him,
And be forever blest.
My darling, Jesus saved thee
From Satan, sin and hell;
And soon with Him in glory,
Forever thou wilt dwell.

Of Jesus' love I've told thee,
I scarce dare tell mine own;
My heart is thine, my darling,
Thine truly and alone.
Unto my heart I'd take thee,
And let thee nestle there;
I'd comfort, I'd console thee,
And breathe thy name in prayer.

Through life I'd be thy stay, love,
Thy solace and thy joy;

In harmony we'd dwell, love,
In peace without alloy.
In death we would not part, love,
Ah, no! we both would rise
To our bright home on high, love,
With Jesus in the skies.

There, to the harps of gold, love,
A glorious song we'd raise;
And with the Lamb we'd reign, love,
And ever sing His praise.
O, take me to thy heart, love,
And let me nestle there!
May all thy paths be peace, love,
And all thy life a prayer.

May, 1858.

ON HEARING A CHILD SING.

To my mind, the best representation of an angel is a beautiful child singing, with pathetic fervor, a hymn that expresses a longing for heaven.   If I close my eyes, I can see her among the undefiled before the throne.

O BLESSED child ! I heard thee breathe
   Melodiously a lay ;
Thy soul was trembling in thy voice,
   My spirit felt its sway.
A gush of holy feeling welled
   Up from my deepest soul,
And rose to ecstasy, as on
   My ear thy warbling stole.

I held my breath, and bowed my head,
   As if I were spell bound ;
Unconscious I became, save of
   A low, soul-thrilling sound.
I was awake, and yet I dreamed,
   Or else my spirit flew,
Upon the wings that Music lent,
   And bathed in heav'nly dew.

November, 1859.

FIRST LOVE LOST.

Incidents in a dream are often as painful or pleasant, and as fully lamented or enjoyed, for the time being, as if they were real. In like manner, he who has a vivid imagination enters wholly into the spirit of his composition, though it be only a creation of fancy.

I HAD a rose, a lovely flower,
It blossom'd once alone for me;
It blooms in peerless beauty still,
Among the roses on the tree.
But no sweet-scented fragrance now
The blooming rose exhales for me;
I see the blushing leaves unfold,
Yet, mine they never more can be.

I had a star, a brilliant gem,
For none but me 'twas wont to shine;
Its light in glory bathed my life,
I proudly said, "The star is mine!"
How oft I raised my raptured eyes,
To view its soul-entrancing light;
I raise them now, alas! the star
Hath disappeared in Hatred's night!

I crowned an idol in my soul,
And worshipp'd at its shrine alone;

God saw the sacrilege; in wrath
He tore the idol from His throne:
In penitence before His feet,
I strove resignedly to bow,
And crush the passion in my heart,
But yet I feel its yearnings now.

The face I loved appears to me
In dreamy hours of silent night;
The vision aggravates my grief,
And yet I weep to see the light;
For dark, expressive eyes meet mine,
And auburn curls droop o'er my brow;
But with the dawn of morn, they fade,
And I am then as I am now.

Of my young heart the pristine love
To one flowed ardently and free;
I fondly hoped it was returned,
For so it truly seemed to be.
My hope is crushed, my heart is lone,
And wonder-stricken in despair;
My too-confiding soul has learned
That woman's not divine, though fair.

Seek not on earth for changeless love,
Or draughts of pleasure unalloyed;
A cup of wine, with poison drugged,
Had better far be unenjoyed.

O Thou! in whom I live and move,
Thou only dost deserve my love;
Supremely may it flow to Thee,
Here, now, and evermore above!

1858—1859.

LITTLE ALICE.

GENTLE, lovely, little Alice,
  Fair as a blooming flower ;
Sweet as a blushing, dewy rose
  Kissed by the summer shower !

Sparkling, sprightly, hopeful Alice,
  Bright as the sunbeam's ray !
Thy dimpling smile is like the light,
  That shineth in the day !

Winning, fairy, fragile Alice,
  Thou art a spotless dove !
Thy mouth is like a fragrant bud,
  Thine eye doth melt in love !

Mourning, weeping, little Alice,
  A rainbow in the cloud !
A twinkling star in evening's sky,
  Wrapt in a fleecy shroud (!)

Guileless, harmless, thoughtful Alice,
  I know thou art too fair
To blossom in a world of sin,
  Without the Saviour's care.

Oh ! may thy tender, loving heart
   To Jesus Christ be given,
And thou wilt bloom forevermore
   A lily fair in Heaven !

March, 1859.

THE PARTING.

We met, we loved, then parted near
 A corner on Life's way,
And ever since we have been sad,
 Though seeming blithe and gay.

Our weeping eye, our whitened cheek,
 And wildly throbbing heart,
Constrained us both in soul to say,
 " 'Tis hard, 'tis hard to part."

" I love thee not," thou saidst, but, oh !
 " I love thee," said thine eye ;
That silent language I believed,
 And shall until I die.

We're parted now, and yet we're joined
 By love's mysterious power ;
We speak not, but our souls commune
 Through many a thoughtful hour.

Mysterious fate ! we're doomed to live
 Asunder and forlorn,
Though Heav'n decreed that we should love,
 Ere ever we were born !

8

To thee, O darling of my heart !
　　My first love hath been given ;
But, lost one, thou wilt surely be
　　Both mine and Christ's in heaven.

December, 1859.

THE RETURN.

When one returns to a much loved object, after a long separation, the first and mutual emotion, when the ecstasy of reunion has subsided, if they both love God, is one of gratitude to Him who has brought them together again. Prayer, in such a moment, is, what it always ought to be, the spontaneous outgoing of the desires and affections toward the Deity.

I HAVE returned, my love,
  And thou dost view
Thy lover, as in seasons past,
  To his love true.
I'm sad and weary, love,
  I fain would rest,
And pillow now this throbbing head
  Upon thy breast.

I have returned, my love,
  O kiss me now !
My lips and eyelids gently press,
  And stroke my brow.
Belovéd, speak to me,
  As when of yore,
Beneath the moon, thou saidst " I'm thine
    Forevermore !"

Gaze fondly on me, love,
   With thy dark eyes,
In whose serenest, liquid depths,
   Love's spirit lies.
O touch me softly, love,
   A passioned thrill
Will vibrate through my deepest soul,
   And my cup fill!

Draw nearer to me, love,
   And let us feel
That mystic fellowship of soul,
   Voiceless, but real.
I know that mine thou art,
   And I am thine,
And we are God's; thus are we linked
   By chains divine.

Give me thy hand, my love,
   Now let us kneel,
And, underneath the eye of God,
   Our troth-plight seal.
Silent we pray; God hears,
   Through His dear Son;
Heav'n whispers to our hearts, we feel
   That they are one.

I have returned, my love,
   But oh! in heaven

None e'er return, for leave to roam
 Is never given ;
And no desire is felt
 To wander thence ;
There will we love, but never part
 When we go hence !

March, 1860.

TO NOBODY.

My Loved One, when the ev'ning shades
　　In silence o'er us fall ;
When twinkling stars in Night's blue vault,
　　To rest and slumber call,
　　　　I'll think of thee.

When dew-bathed roses fall asleep,
　　Hushed by the murm'ring breeze ;
When moonbeams play at "hide and seek,"
　　Among the rustling trees,
　　　　I'll pray for thee.

When, on the starry breast of Night,
　　The earth in stillness lies ;
When lonely woods, and haunted towers,
　　Resound the owlets' cries,
　　　　I'll dream of thee.

When Seraphs draw the shades of Eve
　　Around the setting sun ;
And, through the folds, peep at the earth,
　　To see what they have done,
　　　　Oh! think of me!

My darling, in the hallowed hour
  When fireflies light the dew,
When starbeams glide among the graves,
  And kiss the waters blue,
    Oh! pray for me!

When Angels all thy senses lull
  With drafts of soothing sleep;
And, when thou dream'st of one who loves,
  And who his vows will keep,
    Oh! dream of me!

January, 1860.

PREMONITIONS OF AN EARLY DEATH.

Nearly all young sentimental persons, especially if their health is not robust, imagine that they are fated to die at an early age. They frequently nurse this idea until it becomes the cause of sickness, and even of death, itself. Such persons should retire with a clear conscience, at peace with God and man, sleep soundly, rise early, use plenty of cold water, take long walks, eat heartily of plain, nutritious food, do good, and, finally, be more matter of fact.

SHADES of darkness round me gather,
　　Rising from the tomb,
Veiling all my hopes of glory,
　　Shrouding me in gloom.

Dark Foreboding o'er my spirit
　　Spreads its dreary wings,
While the voice of Premonition,
　　Slow and solemn sings:

" Doomed to die thou art, O mortal,
　　In the morn of Life;
Soon thy soul, in Death's dark valley,
　　Death shall meet in strife.

" Fairest roses fade most quickly,
　　Youth and Beauty die,

Moldering in the silent churchyard,
  Forms like thine do lie !"

Premonition chants ; my spirit
  Quaileth in dismay ;
Shadows shroud my soul, and darken
  Hope's inspiring ray !

Near a black, mysterious river,
  Sad and lone I stand ;
While, before my troubled vision,
  Flits a spectral band !

Stygian shades around me gather,
  Rising from the tomb,
Veiling all my hopes of glory,
  Shrouding me in gloom.

June, 1859.

THE ANGEL AND THE CHILD.

A LOVELY child with dark-blue eyes,
　　And waving, silken hair,
Upon her mother's new-made grave
　　Bowed down her head in prayer.
Her golden curls drooped o'er the sod,
　　Tears filled her eyes of blue ;
She knelt in likeness of a flower
　　Bathed in the sun-lit dew.

Beneath the foaming, restless sea
　　Her father long had slept ;
And o'er his ocean-tomb, the waves
　　A wailing vigil kept.
Her mother lay in Death's embrace,
　　Beneath the churchyard's sod ;
And on her grave the orphan knelt,
　　Before the orphan's God.

She raised her weeping, dark-blue eyes,
　　And whisper'd, "Mother,—come !
I pine, I die for want of love,
　　Oh ! take me to thy home !—
Thy home where Jesus in His arms
　　The lambs doth gently fold ;
Where angels glide in beauty o'er
　　The streets of shining gold !"

Thus spoke the child ; and ere her words
    Had died upon the air,
An Angel stood beside the grave,
    To grant the orphan's prayer !
The Angel parted from her brow
    The waving, golden curls,
And softly kissed away the tears
    That fell, like liquid pearls.

The Angel said, " I'll take thee home,"
    And to her bosom fair
She clasped the child—in light they rose,
    A rainbow in the air !
Down on the grave the orphan looked,
    Upon the grave she smiled ;
Then faded softly from my sight
    The Angel and the child !

February, 1859.

HOPE AND LOVE.

HOPE is an angel from the sky,
   A seraph born above;
She has a sister pure and bright,
   Her sister's name is Love.

Hand clasping hand, these sisters glide
   Throughout this vale of tears;
Love strikes a chord within our hearts,
   Hope dissipates our fears.

When yearning for a kindred soul,
   To fill a void within,
Love openeth our hearts, and draws
   A kindred spirit in.

When clouds of sorrow o'er us hang,
   Hope, like a star, doth rise;
With beaming face, and lifted hand,
   She pointeth to the skies!

When, in the gloomy vale of Death,
   We stand beside the grave,
Then Hope will cheer our fainting hearts,
   And Love our spirits save.

On either side the golden gate,
    Blest Hope and Love will stand,
To welcome all the blood-bought throng
    Into the Promised Land.

But of the sisters, only one
    Will live and reign on high;
For Hope, upon the breast of Love,
    In Paradise shall die.

May, 1859.

THE LITTLE, LAUGHING, BLUE-EYED CHILD.

If anything will touch the heart of a misanthrope, it is the artlessness and the unrestrained affection of a child.

I SADLY wandered forth one day,
And pondered, as I stroll'd along,
On themes distasteful to my heart,
Yet suited to a Poet's song.
I thought of all the glorious hopes
I cherished when my youth began,
Of love's bright dreams which now, alas !
Have faded, like the hopes of man.
I thought of friends whom time had tried,
And proved as treach'rous as the sea ;
Then Memory, grieved, said to my heart,
" Can such a thing as friendship be ?"

The cank'ring love of gold that burns
In many a heart this very day,
Hath poison'd Friendship's sacred fount,
And chased God's angel far away.
Of sympathy for want and woe,
Desire for gain hath robbed the soul ;
O what a heart-enlarging power,
This man-degrading passion stole !

The goddess, Fashion, round the soul
Hath weaved a spirit-wounding spell ;
For when her vot'ries feel love's power,
Of love they must not, dare not tell.
A limpid, gurgling stream that flows
Right freely through a shaded vale,
Discoursing music as it hastes
The weary pilgrim to regale,
Hath on its rippling bosom now
Of rankest poison handfuls strew'd,
The pilgrim drinks to quench his thirst,
But ah ! the draught with death's imbued !
So Fashion poisoneth the stream,
That flows from ev'ry loving heart ;
She turns the simple into guile,
Transforms the artless into art !

"Ah, me!" I said, " the human race
By Gold and Fashion is enslaved ;
The signet of this king or queen,
On ev'ry human heart's engraved."

While thus I mused, I heard a voice,
That sweetly said, " Thou art beguiled ;"
I turn'd I look'd and, lo ! I saw
A little, laughing, blue-eyed child !
Kind glances from her gentle eyes,
Love's halo beaming on her face,
Showed in her sympathetic heart

The love of gold had found no place.
Her simple manner, as she stood
A graceful beauty, unadorned,
Proclaim'd that she had never yet
The arts of formal fashion learned.
The depths of her blue orbs revealed
A nature ardent, pure and mild ;
Oh ! how I wish'd the world was like
This little, laughing, blue-eyed child !

February, 1859.

SPEAK GENTLY.

"O germ! O fount! O word of love!
  O thought at random cast!
Ye were but little at the first,
  But mighty at the last."—MACKAY.

A correct idea of the power of language is seldom entertained. Many of us forget that our conversation—yea, almost every word we utter—exercises a mighty and a lasting influence. We who are Christians, fail to realize the great amount of moral power we might exert by the loving use of encouraging words. We are prone to distrust and shun the penitent profligate, and too apt to turn the "cold shoulder" on the church-member who once yielded to temptation, but who is now confessing his sin, and seeking the forgiveness and favor of God. This course is contrary to the spirit of the Gospel, and to the example of our blessed Saviour. "Neither do I condemn thee; go and sin no more," were the gracious words that fell from the lips of Jesus, like heavenly music, on the ear of the penitent. We, who are too censorious, forget our own liability to fall, and remember not the Apostle's injunction: "Brethren, if a man be overtaken in a fault, ye who are spiritual, restore such a one in the spirit of meekness; considering thyself, lest thou also be tempted."

We may foster good resolutions in a struggling heart by a single word fitly spoken. Sunshine and dew are not greater blessings to the drooping flower, than smiles and gentle words of hope and love to the tempted soul. On the other hand, how many spirits emerging from the gloom

of error and sin into an atmosphere faintly illuminated by
the first rays of truth and holiness—how many spirits be-
ginning to aspire Godward—have been astonished and
wounded by harsh or thoughtless words from an ill-tem-
pered, morose Christian. *An ill-tempered, morose Christ-
ian!* What a contradiction of terms!

Let gentle words—words of admonition, encouragement,
faith and love—fall ever from our lips. Jesus will smile
upon them, and they will be transformed into rays of
spiritual sunshine. Our souls will then be fountains, our
lips outlets, and our words beams of heavenly love and
light. Our own hearts will be cheered, ennobled and
purified, while many among the redeemed, in time and
eternity, will bless the Lord, that He gave us souls in
which Christian thoughts were conceived, and tongues
that uttered gentle words!

SPEAK gently, for an angry word
    May probe a tender part,
And be a keen-edged knife to pierce
    A tempted, struggling heart.
Shades may, or may not cloud the brow,
    Or moisture dim the eyes;
But, hidden in the spirit's depths,
    The word corroding lies.

Speak gently; Jesus never spoke
    In strains of passion wild;
The Saviour's voice was ever heard
    In accents meek and mild.
The flower is shaken from its stem,
    When blighting tempests roll,

So, by an angry word, is crushed
　　An earnest, loving soul.

Speak gently ; like the morning dew,
　　Thy words will rise, and shed
From fragrant clouds, a glorious shower
　　Of blessings on thy head !
Thus, thou mayst cheer a drooping soul
　　For whom thy Saviour died ;
And, blessed thought ! in doing this,
　　Thou cheer'st the Crucified !

1860.

MISCELLANEOUS PIECES.

THE STEAM HORSE.

THE steam horse! the steam horse doth ride
   Right gloriously on in his might;
He flies o'er the iron-bound track,
   His speed almost dazzles the sight.
He never grows lazy or tired,
   But strides like a giant, along;
He pierceth and cleaveth the air
   With his echo-awakening song!

The steam horse! the steam horse heeds not
   The distance most great that divides;
At the thought he contemptuously laughs,
   As mile-stones he, puffing, derides.
He rushes along like the wind,
   His nostrils breathe fire as he goes;
To swallows that skim through the air,
   A challenge he fearlessly throws!

The steam horse! the steam horse appears
   Like a warrior bound to the fight;
A conqueror chasing his foes,
   Who glories himself in their flight.
He never grows lazy or tired,
   But strides, like a giant, along;
He pierceth and cleaveth the air
   With his echo-awakening song!

February, 1859.

STANZAS FOR YOUNG MEN.

Some foolish persons, of both sexes, imagine that there is something shameful and degrading connected with labor; while, in fact, the truest dignity of character is manifested by the man or woman who engages in honest toil. The Patriarchs were farmers; some of the Prophets, they who held the closest communion with God, herded flocks; the Apostles were mostly fishermen, and the blessed Saviour himself, for aught we know to the contrary, labored in the workshop of the carpenter, Joseph.

There is a character, or, more correctly, a *thing*, mean enough to be worthy even of Satan's contempt. It is the indolent, vain, brainless fop, which, like a large monkey finely dressed, struts along our thoroughfares, especially Broadway, with a cigar between its teeth, a cane dangling from its gloved hand, an eyeglass resting on its nose, shining patent boots on its compressed feet, and the end of a white handkerchief peeping from the side pocket of its coat. While such a thing parades the street, its father is often either being ruined, or already bankrupt, dead and buried; and its poor, old mother, and wearied sisters, are frequently toiling their lives away for its support.

Young men of America, and of every land! shun and despise the fop, as you would avoid and scorn the very essence of vanity, and the perfect embodiment of selfishness. Never degrade your manhood by imitating its pernicious example, but glory in honest toil.

A youth should never blush to own
That he has blacked his shoes,

Or sewed a button on his pants,
  When he a maiden woos.

If she would look, because of this,
  Upon him with disdain,
His love for painted, soulless clay
  He should at once restrain.

A youth should never be ashamed
  To labor for his mother,
Or toil throughout the day, to clothe
  His little baby brother.

A manly pride he well might feel,
  To take his father's place,
And banish Want, that seeks to pale
  His sister's rosy face.

Of all the human plants that grow
  Upon an earthly soil,
Give me the honest, fearless youth,
  Who's not ashamed of toil.

In halls, in palaces, on thrones,
  You will not find another
As noble as the *boy*, who toils
  To feed his widowed mother !

April, 1860.

SIGHTS AND THOUGHTS ON BROADWAY.

AN EXTRACT FROM A LONG POEM.

Books exist which are not printed
On cream-laid sheets with gold-gilt tinted ;
Books there be by men unwritten,
And by critic's rod unsmitten.
"This cannot be," you say, " Because
Each book is clutched by critics' claws,
And with eagle-eyes inspected,
And by critic-codes dissected."
Yes, 'tis a literary law,
That ev'ry literary flaw.
Must be outspread to public view,
Because this is the public's due ;
And not for what the critic pockets,
By his " squibs " on " Odes to Lockets."
But if the books of which I write
Were criticised, as well they might,
Critics would shame their own profession,
By *critiques* on their own expression.
Each person hath a wondrous book,
The eyes are chapters, lines, a look ;
The volume's found in ev'ry place,
It is the silent, human face.
A walking library exists,

And he may scrutinize who lists,
The countless, varied books that glide
Along the street—a living tide.
Where'er I roam, I watch and think,
Thus, deeper draughts of wisdom drink
From what I see, and feel, and dream,
Than students who more studious seem.
And so, on many a sunny day,
My studio is on Broadway.
My friend, if you'll not sleep or wink,
I'll tell you what I see and think.

A Wall street broker passes by,
With avaricious, gleaming eye;
His eager glance, and lip compressed,
Reveal a soul that lacketh rest;
A furrowed brow, and hoary hair,
Are his returns for years of care.
To gather gold his life's been spent,
To hoard it now his soul's intent;
And yet the gold he dies to save
Will all be left beside the grave;
And, for a lifetime spent in gloom,
His dust will gain—a marble tomb;
But, when is broken Satan's spell,
Which misers cherish long and well,
The gold (appalling truth to tell!)
Will drag the broker's soul to hell!
Because Jehovah placed him here,

To occupy a nobler sphere ;
To lift his voice against the wrong,
To aid the weak crushed by the strong ;
To bless Humanity that groans
'Neath thousand sin-erected thrones ;
To search for Truth, and plead with Heaven,
Till truth and moral power were given ;
To rend Sin's veil, that hides Truth's light,
And thus illumine Error's night ;
To teach a world that long hath trod
In darkness, of itself and God!

Deathless Soul ! adore not " Mammon ;"
This is naught but Satan's gammon,
Practised on unlucky mortals,
Luring unto Ruin's portals,
Charming *through* Perdition's gateway,
Which, when entered, closeth straightway—
Opens not to spirits ever—
By its silence, whispers—" *Never*,"
To their groanings sounding ever.
To their struggles made to sever
Satan's chains that bind forever,
Ruin's gateway answers—" *Never !*"
There they groan and struggle ever ;
Deathless soul ! serve " Mammon " NEVER !

Ladies sweep, with rustling dresses,
Tiny bonnets, braided tresses,

Along the crowded, gorgeous street,
Bowing to the "swells" they meet;
Whisp'ring, from behind a fan,
Of a noble-looking man,
Who, with beard a goat might envy,
Keen eye "rolling in fine frenzy,"
Golden-headed cane in hand,
And an eye-glass to command
Views distinct of ev'ry thing,
Struts, majestic as a king.

Why do *ladies* promenade?
Fear they that their cheeks will fade?
Walk they in pursuit of health
On the street of pomp and wealth?
Health must move with slowest pace,
If they catch it in the chase!
So much they drag, so much they carry,
That they pant if in a hurry.

Alas! they strive to make a show,
And win, by painted cheeks, a beau;
Or captivate, with clothing fine,
A brainless fop, who fain would shine
Among the crowd of starched-up fools,
Who are not men, *but Fashion's tools;*
Who nurse a hair, while virtue dies;
A moustache trim, while conscience cries
Against the vain desires that make

A man submit to many an ache,
From tightened glove, and pinching boot,
To boast a little hand and foot ;
Against the vanity that rules
With sceptre turning men to fools !

January, 1860.

THE MASSACRE OF SAINT BARTHOLOMEW.

And when he had opened the fifth seal, I saw under the altar the souls of them that were slain *for the Word of God, and for the testimony which they held.* And they cried with a loud voice, saying, How long, O Lord, holy and true, dost Thou not judge and avenge our blood on them that dwell on the earth? And white robes were given unto every one of them, and it was said unto them, that they should rest yet for a little season, until their fellow-servants, also, and their brethren, that should be killed as they were, should be fulfilled.—JOHN.

The fatal hour approached. It was Sunday eve, and just six days after the royal marriage. The Catholic citizens, marked by a white scarf upon the left arm and a white cross upon the hat, were assembled at midnight at the Hôtel de Ville. Twelve hundred arquebusiers were distributed along the Seine, through the streets and in the Huguenot quarter. The Duke of Guise, frenzied with the memory of his father's fate, with hatred for his natural enemies, the heretics, and with ambition, as the great Catholic leader, commanded the deadly brigade. . . .

The fearful parts had all been assigned. The players waited, in mute suspense, the signal stroke of the great clock of St. Germain l'Auxerrois. The secret council were assembled for the last time; the plot was finished; and with suppressed tones and furtive glances, they too listened for the knell of death. The city lay hushed in that oppressive stillness which precedes a hurricane—the victims, in unsuspecting sleep, the executioners on stealthy guard.— *Life and Times of Sir Philip Sydney.*

Now sounds the peal!   A vengeful murd'rous
    cry
Ariseth, clam'ring to the silent sky,
As if the damned had heard the knell,
And, shrieking, burst the gates of hell!

A host of Seraphim, unseen by men,
Descend, swift, noiseless, and, with angel-ken,
Watch, eager for the glorious chance,
To bear a soul to Heav'n from France.

The pious Catholics the work begin,
To rid the world of " heretics " and sin ;
Thus Satan aid to catch the prey,
Which Seraphs came to bear away !

Shrieks, agonizing, rend the midnight air,
And moonbeams shine on dreadful carnage there :
The young, the beautiful, the brave,
Are hurried to a bloody grave !

The spirits of the martyrs, one by one,
Rise to the King of Martyrs—God the Son !
Still from the ground their corses cry ;
O " Harlot, drunk with blood," reply !

The Day of Wrath!—the Judgment!—draweth
    near,
When thou, astonished, pale, appalled with fear,
Shalt view the glorious martyr-throng,
And, *for a moment*, hear their song !

The Vision rises !—From the glance of Heaven,
Like ghostly vapors by a tempest driven,
Thy Popes, Kings, Prelates, Priests, and they
Who wounded Jesus, flee away !

Shriek after shriek to Hills and Rocks arise,
" Fall !—Hide as from the gaze of Jesu's eyes ; "
But, hark !—a voice !—the mountains nod,—
" Depart ! Depart ! accursed of God !"

Exulting Seraphim, the Ransomed band,
And white-robed Martyr-throngs from ev'ry land,
Around the Throne, triumphant, sing,
" So perish all Thy foes, O King !"
1859–1860.

A SACRED SCENE.

Formal prayer—words which are the result of mere habit, and only uttered to pacify conscience—exercises no holy influence upon the soul, and is, in the highest sense, displeasing to God. On the other hand, when the existence and presence of the Deity are fully realized, and the sincere desires of the heart offered up to Him, the soul is strengthened, refined and ennobled, while they who listen are, at least, impressed with the reality and solemnity of prayer.

HE knelt in prayer, and o'er the crowded
    throng
Deep silence reigned, for breathing e'en was
    hushed;
And then in truest adoration bowed
Was ev'ry head.
           His hands to Heav'n were raised,
His eyes upturn'd: the windows of his soul,
Though silent, spoke: their supplicating glance
Shone through his tears, and, voiceless, strove
    with God.
His accents, breathing reverence and awe,
Broke from the deep recesses of his soul,
And, tremulous, rose to Jehovah's Throne.

The kneeling multitude could almost hear
The throbbing of their hearts.

                                        Humanity,
All conscious of its Author's boundless power,
Was lost in awe before the Deity.
The knowledge of Jehovah's presence crept,
In deep-felt silence, through the inmost soul
Of each and all.
                        The speaker's voice more low
Became, and sounded lower still, till to
A thrilling whisper it had died away.
The fountain of his soul had overflowed,
And, in its gush of feeling, drowned his voice;
For there he knelt, his hands to Heav'n out-
        spread,
His eyes uplifted, but his voice had fled!

Some midst the silent throng had bowed their
        heads,
And others turned their glances up to God.
In stillness deep as death they all are bound,
No voice is heard, yet ev'ry spirit prays.

O skeptic (!) come! behold the awful scene!
Survey thy fellow-men, as low they lie
Before the Throne of Heav'n!
                        Say, dar'st thou break
The silence which these conscious souls maintain,
Because the power of the Unseen is felt,
And now believe, or say, "There is no God?"

May, 1859.

CHATTERTON.

The history of that loved and lamented genius is painfully affecting. The thought and poetry of his childhood would honor the maturity of age. He struggled alone with poverty, and endured the sneers of an unappreciating world, and yet his young heart, too soon and bitterly acquainted with sorrows, gave birth to immortal thoughts, the influences of which are still felt. Like the majority of poets, he was despised and neglected in life, but honored and applauded after death. Why must the body of a poet be laid in the dust before the world will study and appreciate the language of his soul?

Chatterton died unattended, an atheist and a suicide, in a dreary garret in the city of London. He lived among a race of cold-hearted, hypocritical religionists, whose lives continually contradicted their profession, and doubtless, he judged Christianity by their imperfection and sin. If " the blood of the martyrs be the seed of the church;" then a nominal Christianity is verily the support of Infidelity.

O CHATTERTON! if thy great intellect had only
    grasped
A true conception of the humble Christian's faith,
And bowed in reverence before its Author—
    God ;
If thou hadst only known Him, whom to know
    aright
Is everlasting life, how changed thou wouldst
    have been!
How changed in life, in death, and in eternity !

Christ would have sympathized when all thy
    hopes were crushed,
For well He knew and deeply felt what anguish
    was.
His love for which thy great, benighted spirit
    longed—
Love vaster than the noblest Poet ere conceived,
Or e'en could comprehend—love worthy of a
    God,
Because unchangeable, most surely would have
    cheered
Thy lonely heart.   And when the selfish, blind-
    ed world
Looked down from fancied heights upon the
    " Bristol Boy,"
Despising all the yearnings of a Poet's soul,
Neglecting all the intellectual powers which
    might,
By wise direction, have achieved such grand
    results,
That e'en the universe of pure Intelligence
Would have been greatly honored, and most
    truly blessed ;
Yea, when unkindness probed thy soul so sensi-
    tive,
Vibrated harshly Nature's harp so finely strung,
Faith in a vital union with the living God,
Through Christ who died upon the Cross for
    human sin,

Would sure from heav'n have brought thee sweet,
    divine support.
Faith would have raised thy thoughts beyond the
    clouds of woe
Which gathered, dark and dismal, o'er thy youth-
    ful head,
Beyond the throbbing of thine orphan-heart, (for
    death
Bereft thee of a father's, then a mother's love,)
And left thee, like a wand'ring star in space,
    alone.
Faith would have shown the land of Rest where
    weary souls,
Who love the Lord, forget amid the glorious
    scenes
The deepest sorrows felt on earth.

                                    Jehovah gave
To thee, my native Isle a priceless gem, and yet
Thou didst despise, or fail to know the precious
    gift
Until its light had disappeared.
                                 His soul, that might
Have drunk deep draughts of joy divine in Para-
    dise,
Is lost forevermore; his soul that might have
    praised,
With all the ransomed hosts of heav'n, redeeming
    love,

Perished, for aught we know, eternally.*

                             Great God!
Perchance the Poet never read Thy word aright,
Or else was blinded by the acts of those who
    preach,
But nullify their preaching by their lives. Thou
    know'st,
And while Thy justice is, Thy mercy's infinite.

---

* It is not, as the reader will observe, asserted, without qualification, that the Poet perished eternally, but it is only affirmed that, for aught we know, his soul was lost. And this conclusion, as a matter of course, is based upon the hypothesis that the doctrines of Christianity, as interpreted by what are named " the evangelical denominations," are divine.

September, 1859.

THE IMMORTALITY OF MAN.

Am I immortal? is it true,
That, in this tenement of clay,
There burns a spark of life divine—
A spark whose light shall ever shine?
When to the sepulchre I'm borne,
When silent in the grave I lie,
When into dust my body turns,
Can it be said—*The light still burns!*
The light of Immortality?

Oh! when I pass away from earth,
Like fleeting shadow from the wall,
Or wave that breaks upon the shore,
Say! *am I lost forevermore?*
Or like the billow that returns
Upon the fast-receding tide,
Shall I not pass the shore of Death,
And in Eternity draw breath?
Yea, in Eternity abide!

Why do I die? and what is death?
Is death the word for lack of breath?
Define the power entitled Life,
Explain the deep, mysterious strife,
That rages fiercely in the soul,

Before life's gushing streamlets roll
Into the everlasting sea
Of fathomless Eternity :—
Reveal the meaning of that strife !

The spirit is the life of man,
The body but the soul's abode,
And, when the spirit must depart,
The body feels death's fatal dart ;
And, when the spirit thence hath flown,
The body cannot live alone ;
It, therefore, struggles, starts, and dies,
But, disenthralled, the spirit flies
Unto the Judgment-bar of God !

When man's frail tenement of clay
Is severed from his spirit's sway,
We lay it in the silent grave,
And from corruption none can save.
His body dies, but not his soul,
For, while eternal ages roll,
In heaven with Jesus it shall reign,
Or live amidst eternal pain—
Yea, live amidst eternal pain !

The ruined spirit's dreadful fate
Is but an everlasting state
Of separation from the Fount
Of bliss and glory paramount.

This state is named Eternal Death,
For, through eternity, a breath
Of heavenly air is never drawn
By any of the Serpent's spawn;
Nor by the doomed, who would not pray
For mercy on Salvation's day.
They're dead to love, to hope, and heaven,
From God by sin they have been driven:
This is the soul's eternal death!

Man is immortal; for he feels
The thought of endless being thrill,
Armed with a strange, convicting power,
Throughout his soul. And, in that hour,
The thought, *I'm like a dog in death,*
That passes, with his dying breath,
To dust and nothing else but dust,
Forbids his being to distrust
The immortality of man.

MAN IS IMMORTAL! In the grave
There rots not all he was before.
Where is the Hope that cheered his mind?
The Faith that made him so resign'd?
The Love that charmed his griefs away?
And is his Memory dead for aye?
Are all the longings that opprest
Hushed into everlasting rest?
Ah, no! flowers bloom before they fade!

We would not wrap a gloomy shroud
Of dreary darkness round the sun;
We would not close the twinkling eye
Of every star in evening sky;
We would not change the glorious light
Into a dismal, hopeless night;
Yet, men exist, who, round the tomb,
Cast shades of deepest, darkest gloom,
By doubting Immortality!

A Rainbow spreads its radiant arch,
That speaks of hope, across the sky;
It beautifies the darkest cloud,
Illumes the coffin and the shroud;
It sheds its radiance on the tomb,
And gently dissipates the gloom,
It touches earth, and reaches Heaven:
This Rainbow is the hope that's given
Of glorious Immortality!

1859–1860.

LIFE.

How much is heard from the pulpit and press concerning the solemnity of death! how little, comparatively, of the responsibility and solemnity of life! It is too frequently forgotten that eternal destiny is determined by the deeds done in the body, and not by the manner of our death.

LIFE is to all a grand reality.
It is more solemn far to live than 'tis
To die, because eternal destiny
Depends upon the spirit of our lives.

Is heav'n to be desired? Hell to be shunned?
Then, heav'n must be secured in life, and hell
Escaped before we die. Must we be saved,
And Jesus glorified? Then, pardon for
Our sins, and grace to live aright, and strength,
To die victorious over death, must be
Obtained HERE, NOW, by vital faith in Christ.
When we are " changed " they cannot be secured,
And while we breathe, and think, and act, we
    die.

As far as the accomplishment of good's
Concerned, the lives of multitudes of men

Are vapor, but the grand results of life
Make life a fact, both awful and sublime.
To live aright is to enjoy God's love,
Which is a heav'n ; but to exist in sin
Incurs His wrath, which is a perfect hell.
To die is but to enter on a state
In which His love or wrath is fully felt.

Life is the portal both of hell and heav'n.
The wicked have a hell within their breast,
The righteous a proemial paradise.
Death fully ushers into either state
Each disembodied soul.
                        Thus, life becomes
To ev'ry member of the human race,
The fount of joy immortal and divine,
Or everlasting woe, the bounds of which
Are God's displeasure, and the spirit's powers.

April, 1860.

                    THE END.

CPSIA information can be obtained
at www.ICGtesting.com
Printed in the USA
BVHW082004120819
555665BV00018B/2134/P